OUR SACRED TRUST

The Spring Arbor University Concept

D1636725

DR. KIMBERLY RUPERT

DR. BRENT ELLIS | DR. DAVID MCKENNA | GREGORY BONTRAGER

Spring Arbor University
106 E. Main St.
Spring Arbor, MI 49283

ISBN 979-8-9853982-2-9 (paperback)

Library of Congress Control Number: 2023917438

*Special thanks to Susan Panak, Robbie Bolton, the SAU Archives, and the
Spring Arbor University Marketing and Communications department.*

www.arbor.edu

CONTENTS

INTRODUCTION TO
SPRING ARBOR UNIVERSITY

ince its founding in 1873, Spring Arbor has offered to all comers an intentional, unequivocal, and unapologetic Christian education. Whether as a seminary (high school), junior college, four-year college, or doctorate-granting university, our purpose has been to educate for Christ and His kingdom from a biblical perspective for learning, life, and society.

To accomplish this purpose, Spring Arbor requires that those who provide our educational offerings – whether trustees, administrators, faculty, or staff – be individually committed to the Christian faith. We accomplish this by careful hiring, annual requirements to affirm our statement of faith, and further occasions for evaluation of our colleagues' Christian convictions. Spring Arbor University is a Free Methodist Church institution guided by John Wesley's own relations with other Christians. Our statement of faith is not narrowly sectarian, although it is consistent with Free Methodist theology. Rather, it sets forth foundational truths embraced by Bible-informed Christians, whatever their denomination.

Our educational offerings are designed to approach all learning through an understanding of Christ as the creator, redeemer, and reconciler of the world, and therefore to address arenas to which God calls His people for resources to meet their needs for service to mankind and for good works for His glory. Our students' professional and personal goals guide both our academic programs and our cocurricular activities. At the same time, we recognize that every Christian is dual vocational in that one is called both to one's economic or societal role and to witnessing in word and deed to the Gospel of Jesus Christ. Therefore, Spring Arbor University seeks to ensure that all our students receive not only the expected mastery of their chosen disciplines but also thorough familiarity with the essentials of the Christian faith. In that way, they are prepared to be kingdom-minded marketplace leaders.

We welcome all who see value in what we teach, and we value each person as made in the image of God and worthy of respect and care in all our interactions. We do not require that our students – whether residential undergraduate, adult certificate seekers, or online graduate students – affirm our statement of faith in order to enroll. We do, however, require conformity to behavioral standards appropriate to a Christian community and an understanding that all instruction will be provided with Christ as the perspective for learning.

When Spring Arbor became a senior college in 1963, we adopted a mission statement known as The Concept. The Concept continues to guide our institution, and we look forward with confidence to its continuing significance and value for the 21st century. In the pages that follow, you will encounter the philosophical and theological underpinnings of our higher education enterprise, a bit of history, and how we seek to accomplish our guiding purpose of educating for Christ and His kingdom. We will explain The Concept and its four components, how we have accomplished those in the past and present, and how we anticipate those commitments shaping the future of Spring Arbor University in the 21st century. We welcome your interest and your potential collaboration in our exciting future.

SESQUICENTENNIAL VISION

Brent Ellis, President of
Spring Arbor University

A pproaching a milestone as significant as a sesquicentennial provides opportunity to reflect upon the achievements, challenges, successes, and failures contained within 150 years of an institution's existence. Perhaps more important and foundational, it provides opportunity to reflect upon purpose and how mission drives movement into the next 150 years. As president of Spring Arbor University, I stand upon the shoulders of many men and women who sacrificed, dreamed, and implemented vision accordingly to meet the challenges that lay before them. I, too, with reliance upon God, confidence in our University Concept, and with the same determination as former leaders to fulfill God's call upon their lives, am committed to provide thoroughly

Christian and academically excellent higher education to any who choose to study at Spring Arbor University.

Today, the landscape of higher education presents numerous challenges. The rising costs of operating a university translate into ever-increasing tuition. Demographic and psychographic shifts within populations decrease the number of students interested in Christian education. Federal and state governments' increasing suspicion of faith-based institutions and the insidious push for pluralism, broadening theological perspectives, and inclusiveness extending well beyond the freedom provided within orthodoxy all present critical challenges for an institution desiring to stand resolutely committed to its founding mission. In the same fashion as the men and women comprising the history of this great institution rose to meet the challenges presented within their day, Spring Arbor University still possesses all things necessary, beginning with our complete and total dependence upon God, to meet the challenges of this day and what may arise during our next 150 years of existence.

When E.P. and Mattie Hart traveled by train to rural Michigan during the winter of 1872 with the intention to establish Spring Arbor Seminary, they could have never imagined Spring Arbor University in its current form outside of one critical aspect: our mission. In this introductory chapter, my intent focuses on exploring why mission and its complete and total understanding and ownership throughout all levels of our university remain foundational as we embark upon our next 150 years of education.

In reflecting upon the unique position we hold as recipients of the tremendous work and investment of the many preceding those of us currently associated with Spring Arbor University, the charge the apostle Paul provided his protégé, Timothy, recorded in I Timothy 6:20-21 stands out. Paul writes: *"Timothy, guard what has been entrusted to your care. Turn away from godless chatter and the opposing ideas of what is falsely called knowledge, which some have professed and in so doing have departed from the faith. Grace be with you all."* The idea communicated by Paul here of *"entrusted to your care"* is a banking term meaning a deposit that has been provided to a person or an institution to be cared for. The person making the deposit owns that which is deposited. The person or institution who receives the deposit does not own that which is deposited but becomes the steward of the deposit, working to ensure its safety and provide for its growth. What Timothy received from Paul was not physical but an idea, a vision, a concept. Timothy received the Gospel message from Paul, who had received it directly from Christ Jesus. What Paul commanded Timothy to do with the Gospel message was to *guard* it. Paul does not ask Timothy to invest it. Paul does not ask Timothy to adapt it. Paul does not ask Timothy to grow it. Paul commands Timothy to *guard* it. Why? Because it is precious and under attack. Paul addresses the risk as he implores Timothy to "turn away from godless chatter and what is falsely called knowledge." The attack on the Gospel message was to pervert the Gospel message with a slightly different variant of the message. The truth was at risk and was under attack by "godless chatter and what is falsely called knowledge." The result of this attack Paul describes by writing, "which some have professed and in so doing have departed from the faith." The consequences of the Gospel message being even slightly modified were catastrophic. Paul commands Timothy to guard the Gospel message because it is precious and under attack.

Similarly, we who have received Spring Arbor University should recognize that we are not the owners of this great institution; we are merely stewards of it. In the same manner Paul entrusted the Gospel message to Timothy, we have been entrusted to care for Spring Arbor University during this unique time in history. While it is tempting to see and understand Spring Arbor University as its student body, our gifted faculty and staff, the wonderful facilities and campus infrastructure, or even the growing endowment, those are merely the byproducts of Spring Arbor University. They are not Spring Arbor University itself. Instead, like the Gospel message, Spring Arbor University is not physical. It is an idea, a vision, a concept. Through the past 150 years, the concept Spring Arbor University employed has produced what we see physically, but Spring Arbor University is not any more physical than the Gospel message. While we do retain responsibility to care for our students, invest in our physical plant, hire and retain gifted employees, and grow our endowment, my conviction remains that our most critical responsibility is to guard the concept of Spring Arbor University that has been entrusted to us. Buildings and infrastructure come and go. Faculty, staff, and, with greater frequency, presidents come and go. Enrollment will fluctuate. What remains and what is worth guarding is our vision, our purpose, our concept. It is under attack and precious, and therefore worth guarding with vigor, commitment, and resolve.

The vision of what is now Spring Arbor University began in the early 1860s, when Rev. Benjamin Titus "B.T." Roberts, a pastor of a Methodist Episcopal Church in New York, began speaking against pew rentals and the distortion of Methodist teaching of salvation, sanctification, and justification. Eventually Roberts was dismissed from the Methodist Episcopal Church and helped found the Free Methodist Church. This new denomination advocated for free pews, the freedom of slaves, the freedom of the Spirit in worship, and other freedoms. B.T. Roberts believed the purpose of the Free Methodist Church was to "maintain the Bible standard of Christianity and to preach the gospel to the poor" (Snyder, pg. 113). B.T. Roberts' commitment to "preach the gospel to the poor" is contextualized by Snyder in *B.T. Roberts Up-to-Date Vision of Earnest Christianity*: "By the 'poor,' Roberts meant 'the masses,' particularly in distinction to 'the rich' who were gaining increased economic and political clout in his day." The idea of "the poor" led to the intentional advocacy for the abolition of slavery and the commitment to free pews within each Free Methodist church sanctuary. In the same way, Free Methodist colleges would be accessible to non-Free Methodist as well Free Methodist students. Just as early Free Methodists were guided by these commitments to maintaining "the Bible standard of Christianity" and "preaching the Gospel to the poor," our colleges and universities employed these commitments in specific and consistent manners. Free Methodist educational institutions focused on providing education grounded in the biblical perspective and available to all who desired this particular approach to teaching and learning.

These two commitments are clearly echoed in the founding documents of Spring Arbor University. In *Concept and Commitment: A History of Spring Arbor University,* Howard Snyder writes: "The Christian faith, and specifically the Bible, were to provide the controlling perspective in the educational program of the school," and, "The school was intended primarily to provide education for the children of Free Methodist families but was to be open to non-Free Methodists also" (pg. 12). The combination of commitment to education from a biblical perspective and being open to any student who desired this approach to education was the hallmark of Spring Arbor Seminary. Snyder also records: "B.T. Roberts announced the fall term of the school at Spring

Arbor in the 1873 issue of the Earnest Christian, noting that the aim of both Spring Arbor and Chili Seminary in New York was to 'combine sound and thorough scholarship with careful religious training'" (pg. 11). The vision of the emerging school was clear: provide academically rigorous education from an unapologetically biblical perspective to any person who desired this type of educational approach.

The commitment to access in higher education truly was a differentiating thought at the time. When the majority of Christian institutions of higher education educated only individuals from their particular denominational persuasion, Free Methodists held to the commitment that anyone could enroll at their institutions. This did not, however mean that non-Christian students would be exempt from religious exercises and experiences. As noted by Snyder in *Rooted in Mission*, during the 1903 Free Methodist General Conference, David Warner, the principal of Spring Arbor Seminary, explained the need for investment into Free Methodist educational institutions. Snyder writes:

> "The purpose constantly has been that schools established and maintained under (Free Methodist) direction should be centers of holy influence and spiritual power, that scriptural holiness should be the watchword, and that from these centers should be sent forth men and women with trained minds, full of faith

and of the Holy Ghost, 'to contend earnestly for the faith once delivered to the saints.'" (p. 79)

Even for entering non-Christian students, the desired outcome was a graduate committed to the Christian faith and prepared to impact the world for Christ and His Kingdom. B.T. Roberts articulated this commitment in his article *Christian Schools* in an 1884 issue of the *Earnest Christian.* Roberts writes that the "result that is especially aimed at is to train these boys and girls for happiness here; and for glorious immortality hereafter ... To imbue them thoroughly with Christian principles and make them accustomed to Christian practices; in short to do all that can be done to help them to become intelligent, educated, consistent, efficient Christians." While admitting non-Christian students into Spring Arbor Seminary was intentional, so would be the curriculum and desire to see all graduates come to faith and be prepared to act as ambassadors of Christ within the world. The purpose was to provide thoroughly Christian and academically excellent education to any who choose to study at Spring Arbor.

As Spring Arbor Seminary became Spring Arbor High School, this vision did not change. As Spring Arbor High School became Spring Arbor Junior College, this vision did not change. In the mid-1960s, a young president who graduated from Spring Arbor envisioned a new application of the same vision. In 1960, Dr. David McKenna oversaw

Spring Arbor College's first Higher Learning Commission accreditation and our move to a baccalaureate granting institution. With this shift in application, the Spring Arbor Concept was coined.

> ***Spring Arbor University is a community of learners distinguished by our lifelong involvement in the study and the application of the liberal arts, total commitment to Jesus Christ as the perspective for learning and critical participation in the contemporary world.***

Clearly, the founding tenets articulated by B.T. Roberts and E.P. Hart are contained in the Spring Arbor University Concept and were beautifully applied as Spring Arbor transitioned to a baccalaureate granting institution. Consider these statements from our founders and their linkage to the Spring Arbor University Concept:

- *"The Christian faith, and specifically the Bible, were to provide the controlling perspective in the educational program of the school" (E.P. Hart, 1873).*
- *The purpose of Spring Arbor Seminary was "to combine sound and thorough scholarship with careful religious training" (B.T. Roberts, 1873).*
- *"The purpose constantly has been that schools established and maintained under (Free Methodist) direction*

> *should be centers of holy influence and spiritual power, that scriptural holiness should be the watchword, and that from these centers should be sent forth men and women with trained minds, full of faith and the Holy Ghost, to 'contend earnestly for the faith once delivered to the saints'" (David Warner, Spring Arbor Principal, 1903).*

- *"No process of education is worthwhile which is not founded on Christ and the Bible. Yea, Jesus Christ is the chief cornerstone on any true system of education. He is the embodiment of Truth ... Christian education then demands first of all the Bible as the foundation of all treatises on science, morals, and religion" (Henry Steward, Spring Arbor Principle, 1923).*

Within these statements an intentional community is articulated: **Community of Learners**. Study and God-honoring application of learning is clear: **Study and Application of the Liberal Arts**. The Bible serving as the perspective for learning stands out: **Total Commitment to Jesus Christ as the Perspective for Learning**. Finally, there is a call for graduates to "contend earnestly for the faith": **Critical Participation in the Contemporary World**. The Spring Arbor University Concept provides a consolidation of the various founding principles of our institution, but it does not vary from this central theme: to provide a thoroughly

Christian and academically rigorous education to any who choose to study at Spring Arbor University.

The Spring Arbor University Concept provides the central mission of Spring Arbor. The four pillars of our Concept are inscribed not only at the center of our campus upon the majestic McKenna Carillon Tower but upon the hearts of the students, alumni, faculty, staff, administrators, and board members.

We are a ***community of learners***. Learning should not merely be the objective of our university students. Understanding the process of learning exists and extends throughout the totality of an individual's life. All of us who make up Spring Arbor University are learners who are curious and seek greater understanding of the world in which we live. We are all learners gathered into our university community. This community, while centered in Spring Arbor, Michigan, extends globally to our faculty, students, alumni, and board members who are scattered around the world. In no way diminishing those gathered within our campus, our ***community of learners***, like our mission, is beyond a physical space. Community exists and manifests itself wherever Spring Arbor-related people seek greater understanding of our God and of our world through the process of learning.

We are ***distinguished by our lifelong involvement in the study and the application of the liberal arts***. Undergirding ***community of learners***, this second pillar

15

of our Concept expresses the lifelong pursuit of learning. Spring Arbor University is not interested merely in teaching students what to think but how to think and how to learn. Study then becomes a lifelong endeavor. Coupled with study is a critical aspect of our Concept: application. It is not enough to know the content of a particular subject. It's necessary to understand how to best utilize and apply that knowledge. It is the difference between wisdom and knowledge. Spring Arbor University desires the members of our community to move beyond knowledge and into wisdom, the appropriate and God-honoring application of knowledge. Liberal arts education provides the most effective tools in aiding students in this type of learning. Even within professional programs like business, education, social work, nursing, and engineering, students' learning begins with a foundation of the liberal arts. Our graduates do not merely know their discipline but also understand how to apply their learning because they know how to learn, how to think, how to communicate, how to problem solve, and how to work collaboratively. All of this is the byproduct of a liberal arts education.

A total commitment to Jesus Christ as the perspective for learning provides the most distinctive and critical component of our Concept. Notice our Concept does not say "a" perspective but "the" perspective. This particular use of the article "the" provides a powerful statement about our unique approach to education. If indeed there is a God that exists that created all that exists with intentionality and purpose, and if this creator God, in order to save his creation, sent his Son to redeem the world and desires to make his love, grace, and mercy known to all people through those who have accepted his free gift of salvation, then it should radically shift the orientation and purpose of all individuals and institutions. Therefore, we do not say "a" perspective but "the" perspective, because we are convinced removing God from the exploration of learning limits our ability to understand truth. A person may be able to understand facts about a given topic without an understanding of God, but that person will never be able to move to a broader understanding of truth. Take, for example, the digital code. The sequencing of 0's and 1's provides access to information in manners and ways that amaze all. While people can learn the facts about the digital code that allow the functional use of the digital code without foundationally understanding why it works, that prevents them from arriving at truth. Approaching the digital code with Christ as the perspective for learning begins with an understanding of God and his creation. We live in a world that is observable, measurable, and repeatable. We possess confidence that when two parts hydrogen is put together with one part oxygen the result will always be water. When we place a particular sequence of 0' and 1's together, the result, likewise, will always be the same. Our world is built upon such confidence in the repeatable aspects of what we can observe and measure. We have this confidence because we know God intentionally created the world in this manner. God desires us to be curious, to learn, to have dominion over his creation. As Christians, we never need to fear inquiry. The deeper we delve into a subject the more we understand the mind of our Creator and his purposes for us in this world.

Critical participation in the contemporary world concludes our Concept with a call for the application of our learning and our curiosity. It is not enough to possess knowledge. The call of God upon our lives is to act within our world in a manner and way that applies learning and knowledge in redemptive and reconciliatory manners. The call of God is to apply learning in manners that impact the world for Christ and His kingdom. One of my favorite examples of an alumnus living this out is Dr. Robert Gould. Dr. Gould once told me that as he reflected upon this pillar of our Concept as a student that he understood his role as a research scientist was to do all he could to reverse the consequences of the fall of humanity through drug manufacturing. This led Dr. Gould to spend most of his career discovering and producing drugs to fight AIDS, genetic cancers, and genetic diseases like Sickle Cell Anemia and Muscular Dystrophy. Our community members, scattered throughout the world, who are living and acting as critical participants in the contemporary world, are humbling to consider. James 5:20 states: "Consider this, whoever brings back a sinner from his wandering will save his soul from death and will cover over a multitude of sins." It is staggering to consider the multiplicative effect the Spring Arbor community has had on our world with our 70,000 alumni acting as critical participants in the contemporary world. Not everyone cures diseases and not everyone leads another to Christ. But the cumulative impact of our community of learners upon our world when we individually and corporately live as critical participants in the contemporary world is truly unmeasurable.

Spring Arbor University is this vision, this idea, this concept. The thread, woven throughout our amazing history, is providing a thoroughly and unapologetically Christ-centered, biblical perspective of rigorous education to any and all who desire. As Paul implored Timothy to guard what had been entrusted to him, we too are responsible to guard this precious mission. We guard it because it is precious and because it is at risk. At risk because of the challenges facing higher education. At risk because of the push to blur the lines between being broadly ecumenical and pluralistic. At risk because as we stand for the biblical standard of Christianity broader society and culture may not understand us. Nonetheless, we guard it because it is precious. Precious because it glorifies our God. Precious because it honors all people as image bearers of God. Precious because it transforms individual lives. Precious because it provides the training and growth for those transformed lives to go and impact our world for Christ and His kingdom.

Our purpose and that for which we have been entrusted by all who have come before us is to educate for Christ and His kingdom and advance the biblical perspective in learning, life, and society to all who desire.

SPRING ARBOR UNIVERSITY'S
FOUNDING PRINCIPLES

⸻

The second half of the 19th century in America was a time of reevaluation of the Christian faith. Liberalism, then known as Modernism, questioned the authority of the Bible. The emphasis on revivalism from earlier in the century diminished confidence in doctrine compared to experience. At the same time the social gospel movement emphasized good works over good theology. The Civil War had disturbed the national confidence in the postmillennial expectation of increasing spiritual progress. Meanwhile, material progress brought greater focus on occupational training and worldly success. Further, immigration brought non-Protestant understandings of the faith into greater prominence. Finally, expansion of the population westward brought both spiritual and educational challenges of serving a larger and larger geography.

Various denominations sought to provide Christian education in these new circumstances and new territories. They particularly saw the need for higher education addressing the expanding information and training requirements of the new economy, provided in the context of the traditional understandings of the faith. The Free Methodist Church (FMC) also saw this need and embarked upon a campaign of establishing a network of schools eventually reaching from New York to California and Washington state. Spring Arbor was the second school established by the FMC.

Three distinctives characterized the Free Methodists. First was a commitment to the authority of Scripture and to implementing its teachings in the world. It was this that led to the formation of the church by abolitionists, separating from other Methodists who supported slavery. Free Methodists were and are convinced that every person is made in the image of God and therefore worthy of respect, dignity, and freedom from oppression. In addition, they believe that every individual is equal before God and therefore worthy of receiving whatever services the church might offer. In the early days, this was most evidenced by elimination of pew rents, which had prevented the poor from participating in worship services. Second, in common with the Protestant view of work, all callings and occupations were viewed as means to serve and glorify God. Therefore, consistent with the broader Wesleyan tradition, Free Methodists emphasized the value of education, both "secular" and religious, for all persons but particularly for Christians so that they might have means to meet their own needs and to serve others, not least by sharing the gospel. A third distinction, evidenced by affiliation with the Holiness movement, was a confidence in God as the source of life and therefore of standards for living rather than looking to society for such guidance.

Perhaps the greatest gift early Free Methodism provided its churches and educational institutions centered on the foundational aspects of the denomination "to maintain the Bible standard of Christianity and to preach the gospel to the poor." This statement, recorded by B.T. Roberts, the founder and first general superintendent of the Free Methodist Church, in his periodical *The Ernest Christian* and quoted by Howard Snyder in his book, *Rooted in Mission: The Founding of Seattle Pacific University 1891-1916*, provides a coherent understanding of the purpose of Free Methodism and its associated institutions. Snyder unfolds these two foundational commitments in his article *B.T. Roberts Up-to-Date Vision of Earnest Christianity*:

> "Based on Jesus' example and teaching, the church's primary mission is to 'preach the Gospel to the poor' and 'to maintain the Bible standard of Christianity.' This meant, especially, evangelism among the masses, particularly the poor and oppressed; the building of a community of believers among

23

those who respond; the church's continuing mission to reach the poor; and doctrine tested by Scripture."

"The poor" referenced the disenfranchised in whatever arena. In the educational arena, that meant that education was not to be limited to "approved" groups only but for all who might benefit thereby.

As these commitments guided early Free Methodists, they sought to reach the world for Christ through the development of Christian educational institutions. While our founders understood the uniqueness of a church ministry versus an educational institution's mission and purpose, our colleges and universities employed these two commitments in specific and consistent manners. Free Methodist educational institutions focused on providing rigorous academic education grounded in the biblical perspective and the liberal arts, and on making it available to all who desired this particular approach to teaching and learning.

At the same time, the willingness to teach all comers and the desire that biblical orthodoxy in instruction would not be "narrowly sectarian" and should not be misconstrued to imply openness to all persuasions of scholarship and religious conviction.

John Wesley addresses this misperception in his sermon on the *Catholic Spirit*. In the sermon, Wesley clearly makes the point that catholic Christians should not believe only their particular mode of worship, church governance, baptism, and the like are Christian. Rather, Wesley encourages a broader view of Christian fellowship extending beyond denominational lines. He writes:

> "I ask not, therefore, of him with whom I would unite in love, Are you of my church, of my congregation? Do you receive the same form of church government, and allow the same church officers, with me? Do you join in the same form of prayer wherein I worship God? I inquire not, Do you receive the supper of the Lord in the same posture and manner that I do? nor whether, in the administration of baptism, you agree with me in admitting sureties for the baptized, in the manner of administering it; or the age of those to whom it should be administered...Let all these things stand by: we will talk of them, if need be, at a more convenient season, my only question at present is this, 'Is thine heart right, as my heart is with thy heart?" (paragraph I, 11) *sic*

Later within this same sermon, Wesley clearly communicates that while breadth of opinion on some subjects is appropriate, openness to opinions and ideas not consistent with the character and the will of God that is articulated in scripture is "the spawn of hell." He writes:

> "For...a catholic spirit is not speculative latitudinarianism. It is not an indifference to all opinions: this is the spawn of hell, not the offspring of heaven. This unsettledness of thought, this being 'driven to and fro, and tossed about with every wind of doctrine,' is a great curse, not a blessing, an irreconcilable enemy, not a friend, to true catholicism. A man of a truly catholic spirit has not now his religion to seek. He is fixed as the sun in his judgment concerning the main branches of Christian doctrine." (paragraph III, 1) *sic*

Commitment to the Bible standard of Christianity is directly tied to John Wesley's understanding of the supremacy and authority of the Bible. Wesley is famous for claiming to be a man of one book. In Wesley's Journal entry from June 5, 1766, he writes, "My ground is the Bible. Yea, I am a Bible-bigot. I follow it in all things, both great and small" (p. 251). Wesley understood the importance of human reason and philosophical thought, but he continuously taught that the Bible alone should provide definitions of morality and Christian character. In Wesley's sermon, *The Witness of our Own Spirit*, he states:

"But the Christian rule of right and wrong is the word of God, the writings of the Old and New Testament; all that the Prophets and 'holy men of old' wrote 'as they were moved by the Holy Ghost;' all that Scripture which was given by inspiration of God, and which is indeed profitable for doctrine, or teaching the whole will of God; for reproof of what is contrary thereto; for correction of error; and for instruction, or training us up, in righteousness. (2 Timothy 3:16.) This is a lantern unto a Christian's feet, and a light in all his paths. This alone he receives as his rule of right or wrong, of whatever is really good or evil." (paragraph 6)

Implicit within Wesley's writing is a commitment to allow the clear teaching of the Bible to provide the boundaries for understanding morality and the will of God. Thus, like John Wesley and B.T. Roberts, Free Methodist colleges and universities are ecumenical in spirit, but they are not pluralistic as though non-Christian faiths and non-biblical perspectives offer equivalent access to truth and to God.

Early Free Methodists, then, desired to provide rigorous academic education from the biblical perspective. Howard Snyder reports in *Concept and Commitment*, "B.T. Roberts announced the fall term of the school at Spring Arbor in the September 1873 issue of the Earnest Christian, noting the aim of both Spring Arbor and North Chili Seminary in New York was to 'combine sound and thorough scholarship with careful religious training.'" (pg. 11)

Similarly, Snyder records in *Rooted in Mission*:

> "The most obvious and determining factor in Seattle Seminary's founding and early decades was its explicit, unapologetic Christian commitment. Every articulation of the school's purpose stressed that this was a Christian school. The Christian faith that birthed the institution was a matter of doctrine, ethics, and worship – earnestly committed Jesus-centered life in private, in Christian Community, and in the larger culture." (p. 113)

According to Howard Snyder's essay, *"B.T. Roberts and the Founding of Roberts Wesleyan College,"* Ellen Roberts believed "it was not enough for [students] to maintain a profession of religion, but they must receive the outpouring of the Spirit again and again." While Free Methodist institutions were intended to be nonsectarian, they were indeed intended to be thoroughly and unapologetically Christian, where the biblical perspective in teaching and learning guided all pedagogy. Snyder again writes related to the founding of Spring Arbor, "The Christian faith, and specifically the Bible, were to provide the controlling perspective in the educational program of the school" (p. 12). This commitment echoes B.T. Roberts' desire for the Free Methodist Church "to maintain the Bible standard of Christianity" as well as John Wesley's perspectives of the true catholic faith and the authority of the Bible.

This commitment was joined to the understanding that Free Methodist colleges would be accessible to non-Free Methodist as well Free Methodist students. Recorded in the 1871 minutes of the Michigan Conference of the Free Methodist Church was a statement regarding this commitment: "The most perfect religious toleration shall be observed, and no student shall be deprived of any of the advantages of said school or be in any manner proscribed while attending the same, on account of religious convictions and beliefs" (p. 43). At the same time, as noted by Snyder in *Rooted in Mission* in 1903, David Warner, the principal of Spring Arbor Seminary, explained that:

> "The purpose constantly has been that schools established and maintained under (Free Methodist) direction should be centers of holy influence and spiritual power, that scriptural holiness should be the watchword, and that from these centers should be sent forth men and women with trained minds, full of faith and of the Holy Ghost, 'to contend earnestly for the faith once delivered to the saints'" (p. 79).

This remains the bedrock foundation of Spring Arbor University.

SPRING ARBOR HISTORY FROM
SEMINARY TO THE CONCEPT

⁕

The Free Methodist Church was established in 1860 in Pekin, New York, under the leadership of Benjamin Titus Roberts, who had been expelled from the Methodist Episcopal Church because of his abolitionism. The new church quickly became active in evangelism. In 1863, Edward Payson Hart was an evangelist in Michigan. Ten years later, he was the founder of a seminary, then considered a school of higher education, in Spring Arbor, Michigan. The original 1873 Articles of Association still resound in today's University.

Convinced that "Religion, Morality and Knowledge are essential to good Government and the real happiness of mankind," the founders intended the school to be "an institution of learning wherein young persons may be … instructed in the various branches of learning which tend to fit and qualify them to properly discharge in the future the multifarious duties of good citizenship." Note that the seminary was open to "young persons" and not restricted to men. In addition, according to the original agreement with the Spring Arbor residents, "No student shall be deprived of any of the advantages of said school, or be in any manner proscribed while attending the same, on account of his religious convictions or belief."

The original intent of the school, as derived from founding documents and summarized in Snyder's "100 Years at Spring Arbor" (pp.17-18), might be called the original Spring Arbor concept:

1. The school was to provide a general liberal arts education of high quality. It was not intended to be a theological school but was intended to prepare Christian youth in general to lead constructive lives in society.
2. The school was intended primarily to provide education for the children of free Methodist families but was to be open to non-free Methodists.
3. The Christian faith, and specifically the Bible, were to provide the controlling perspective in the educational program of the school.
4. The school was intended to provide and maintain an environment conducive to serious study inconsistent with Christian living as defined by the Free Methodist church.

5.   The school was to be controlled by an independent board of trustees and thus only loosely affiliated with the Free Methodist denomination. In fact, the first board consisted of seven Free Methodists (four clergy and three laymen) and four non-Free Methodists.

The catalog for 1877-78 offered "the opportunity to secure a good, practical education, combined with careful discipline … as well as due respect for all; and we shall especially endeavor to exhibit the power of Christianity, by precept and godly example." In its first 20 years, the seminary had an average enrollment of 100 or so and produced 79 graduates.

The years around the turn of the century were financially challenging since the school relied entirely on student fees and occasional contributions, but encouragement came with the first endowment, the 1895 Selina Lockwood fund for scholarships for "indigent students preparing for the ministry." DeForrest Gaffin, a dedicated fundraiser, also engendered greater interest among Free Methodist Churches and established the tradition of acknowledging donors with markings in the campus walkways. Enrollment grew, and the future looked promising.

But the founding purpose and perspective of the school had not changed. In 1923, then Principal H. S. Stewart declared in the *Echo*, the school's yearbook:

"Education is for social efficiency; good citizenship; intelligent and useful membership in society ... No process of education is worthwhile which is not founded on Christ and the Bible. Yea, Jesus Christ is the cornerstone of any true system of education. He is the embodiment of all Truth ... Any moral system that leaves Christ out of its reckonings will be a miserable mockery to the soul... True science, morality and religion have their Alpha and Omega in Jesus Christ."

Merlin G. Smith, the first Spring Arbor administrator with a doctoral degree, became the first President (so designated) of Spring Arbor Seminary in 1926 when he was 32 years old. He inherited a debt of $21,000, which was paid off by 1929 through the efforts of John A. Kelley, who was also able to attract estate giving. This was supplemented by increased earnings from the Seminary's farm. The Board of Trustees had voted in 1923 to begin a junior college, which was launched under Smith's leadership in 1928 with a class of 12 college freshmen. Total enrollment reached 287 in 1929-30. The high school continued to attract students, but the primary and intermediate departments were discontinued in 1930. Their facilities were donated to Spring Arbor and became the site of today's Warner Elementary School.

The Great Depression began in 1929, but its effects reached Spring Arbor slowly. A much more threatening event was the December 1930 destruction by fire of the school's chapel and dormitory. The damages totaled $40,000, but the rebuilding effort was estimated at $125,000 to include expanded dormitories, especially for female students. Fundraising efforts were launched but clearly hampered by the Depression. Enrollment also fell, decreasing anticipated income. Consideration was given to merging with another Free Methodist school, either Roberts Wesleyan or Greenville. Moving to Marshall, Michigan, a wealthier town, was also explored. But both faculty and trustees felt that the school's founding and continuance at Spring Arbor "were divinely ordered and guided."

In March 1932, the Board of Trustees voted to stay in Spring Arbor and to adopt whatever belt-tightening measures were necessary. This included a 25 percent decrease in faculty salaries. Salaries more than once went unpaid. One instructor received $50 for the entire year; another cashed in his life insurance policy to live. This period was one of intense and intentional support for each other within the Spring Arbor Junior College community. In May 1932, President Smith moved to become President of Roberts Wesleyan, where he served until 1957.

Things began to improve financially beginning with fundraising efforts by the alumni association beginning in 1933. Two creditors sued the school for unpaid bills. A trustee took personal responsibility until the balance could be paid by himself and with alumni funds. By 1937, Spring Arbor was out of debt.

The Junior College became the focus of Spring Arbor's educational programs. Junior College catalogs from 1935 to 1960 stated three purposes: preparation for those intending to complete bachelor degrees, practical courses for those not anticipating further academics, and training for those called to Christian service. Enrollment expanded, and 734 students graduated from these programs between 1935 and 1957. Major buildings were constructed, and the campus tripled in size with the purchase in 1954 of 27 acres from the Ogle family. Athletic programs expanded after 1943, when the Free Methodist Church General Conference approved intercollegiate competitions for its schools. Donald McDonald led high school teams in track and basketball to multiple championships, and junior college cross country teams under Kenneth Beardslee set a new national record for competition wins.

Faith was not neglected. Dr. Leroy Lowell, President from 1935 to 1944 and 1955 to 1957, set forth his three fundamentals of education: Belief, Character, and Experience:

> "Our belief about things is our philosophy concerning the world in which we live. If God and Christ are left out of our world, we are

not using all the facts. No philosophy of life is adequate which does not account for all the facts. And so true education must be Christian in content. It must have more than a religious flavor or even a religious emphasis – it must be Christ centered ...

Character... What is the chief end of education? That question can be answered when we find the answer to another. What is the supreme end of life? It seems to me that there can be only one answer – character ... The glory of human character is ... our ability to will with God. ... How essential, then, is the education of the heart and conscience as well as the mind.... Increase in power is safe only when it is matched with high ideals ....

Experience ... The *summum bonum* of life is likeness to God, and we would add, that likeness is realized in Jesus Christ. This is not achieved as a result of some educational process ...but education must make a place for the fact of such an experience to the reality of which many in all ages have given clear testimony. Furthermore, I believe that an education which is definitely Christian will prepare the way for that experience."

In 1947, "seminary" was dropped from the school's name, and so became Spring Arbor Junior College. Full accreditation was granted by the state of Michigan in 1951. Three years later, the Trustees undertook a study of future development. In 1956, the Michigan Commission on College Accreditation advised the school to seek regional rather than state accreditation. The required self-study was undertaken by Dean David L. McKenna. Meanwhile, President Roderick J. Smith strengthened the school's administrative structure. McKenna was named Dean of Academic Affairs; Kenneth Beardslee became Director of Business Affairs; and The Director of Student Affairs responsibilities fell initially to Harold Darling. Charles Williams became Director of Public Affairs and Vice President for Development until 1964, winning major grants for the school's ambitions.

The first step to becoming a senior college was achieving full regional accreditation for the Junior College. The required self-study engaged 10 committees of 20 faculty and administrators and was presented to the North Central Association in 1958. Although the study was well received, weaknesses in finances and faculty caused concern. To give Spring Arbor time to shore up those areas, North Central delayed its usual campus visit for one year. Charles Williams' efforts were successful, notably through a fund drive among alumni. In 1959, the Board of Trustees committed the college to developing a four-year liberal arts program and decided that 1960-61 should be the last academic year of

Spring Arbor High School. Finances, faculty, and enrollment improved significantly, and full regional accreditation was granted in April 1960. In May 1960, the school's name was changed to Spring Arbor College.

But what were to be the character and mission of Spring Arbor College, and who should lead it? David McKenna had left Spring Arbor in 1960 for a position at Ohio State and had subsequently accepted a position at the University of Michigan. Nonetheless, Hugh White, Chairman of the Spring Arbor Board of Trustees, reached out to him with the invitation to become the College's President. He was released from his commitment to the University of Michigan and returned to Spring Arbor to lead the institutional process of determining and articulating its purpose. The founding and subsequent statements of purpose were studied to ensure fidelity to the past and application to the present and future. The initial statement of purpose for Spring Arbor College, produced in 1962, stated:

> "Spring Arbor College is an evangelical Christian college. It is a *college* because the faculty and students are actively involved in the quest for knowledge in the major fields of human learning. It is a *Christian college* because the life of learning among the faculty and students is ever held within the perspective of their commitment to the redemptive love

of Jesus Christ. It is an *evangelical Christian college* because the learning and love of faculty and students is aligned with the responsibility of the Christian to be an effective witness in his chosen vocation and a critical participant in his society."

A more succinct statement was first published in the college catalog in 1963. After some further thinking, revisions, and edits, the Spring Arbor mission statement, now known as The Concept, emerged. Spring Arbor College (and now University) is:

A community of learners distinguished by our lifelong involvement in the study and application of the liberal arts, total commitment to Jesus Christ as the perspective for learning, and critical participation in the contemporary world.

The Planks of The Concept

A community of learners distinguished by our lifelong involvement in the study and application of the liberal arts, total commitment to Jesus Christ as the perspective for learning, and critical participation in the contemporary world.

The Concept and its four components, or "planks," have guided Spring Arbor as it has grown from Spring Arbor College to Spring Arbor University. They have provided a rudder as we have navigated significant changes in American higher education in general and Christian higher education in particular. At 60 years old, The Concept is one of the older mission statements among American colleges and universities today. Much has changed, including how The Concept can be understood and applied to new circumstances and challenges. Is it still relevant and powerful for today and for the 21st Century?

To answer that question, it is well to consider each plank, what it has meant, and what it can mean.

A COMMUNITY OF LEARNERS

A COMMUNITY

What is meant by community, particularly three critical aspects of community in Christian higher education: social, scholarly, and spiritual?

Often when people think about community, they think in the first instance about the social component. To be sure, Spring Arbor has a longstanding tradition of mutual care within our community. In its earliest years, virtually all employees lived near to the campus. They often attended the Spring Arbor Free Methodist church adjacent to the campus. Faculty frequently dined with students or entertained them in faculty homes. Faculty themselves frequently socialized and looked out for each other. This was perhaps most evident during the Great Depression, when those employees who had been paid would assist families awaiting payment in the next pay period. All felt a great sense of ownership and responsibility for the school and for their colleagues and students. This sense of community continues, not least in the remarkable number of Spring Arbor's multigenerational legacy students and employees.

Even as the enrollment of the school grew and employees moved further away from campus, the close focus on undergraduate residential students created an intense sense of social community. To many who first encounter the Spring Arbor Concept, it appears that "community" in the social sense, particularly as identified with the longest serving employees of the university, is the primary definition of community within The Concept. Even as other components of community are identified as important, the social aspect does not lose its legitimate importance within the university.

When The Concept was written, Spring Arbor's community consisted of students on campus and faculty and staff living for the most part near the campus. Although most of our students were drawn from rural Michigan, we welcomed international students as early as 1903 with the arrival of Peter Magubeni from South Africa. The diversity of our community expanded as Olive Johnson, our first African American student, enrolled in 1920.

Also, then as now, our community extended to alumni, trustees, donors, and supporters who often played critical roles in shaping Spring Arbor and helping weather difficult times. Our alumni and advancement activities do result in financial support to the University, but our motivation is the conviction that God has developed areas of interest and passion among our alumni and potential supporters. Therefore, we seek to provide to them opportunities at Spring Arbor that may provide a means for them to act upon their interest or passion so as to participate in our purpose of educating for Christ and His kingdom. In this way, they become friends and integral members of our Spring Arbor community.

Today, most of our students are not on campus, and our faculty include full-time and adjunct instructors throughout the country. Approximately 40 years ago, Spring Arbor began to offer degree completion programs to adults in face-to-face classes at sites around Michigan. Great emphasis was placed on creating belonging and community at those sites, with considerable success. These efforts included not only full-time staff persons assigned to each site but also encouraging class members to share meals, studies, and personal concerns – all with considerable success.

Spring Arbor was also an early entrant into online learning to accommodate our remote students. We experienced rapid growth in new online degree programs while seeing a decline in general demand for site-based offerings. Further, the Covid-19 pandemic accelerated adoption of Zoom instruction, both as an alternative to face-to-face and as a complement to existing online classes. In all cases, we continue to seek actively to build student engagement and belonging through such means as group assignments and Spring Arbor campus residencies.

Although some schools chose to separate their off-campus and campus-based faculties, Spring Arbor chose to place responsibility for all discipline-related instruction under a single department for that field. This ensures that a Spring Arbor education is a Spring Arbor education wherever and however received. It also enables a close association of remote and campus faculty and staff. Organization of departments into schools further encourages community through interdisciplinary collaborations.

Beyond the social aspect, as suggested immediately above, scholarship as community is also of great importance. Spring Arbor University takes its identity as an educational institution most seriously. Part of that mandate is obviously ensuring that our faculty are current within their disciplines and fully prepared to teach those disciplines to our students. Toward that end, the university provides support for scholarly activities of our faculty and encourages opportunities to share research with the community through individual presentations, such as our "Community of Learners" lectures, and annual collective consideration of key issues through our FOCUS programs. Faculty also are supported in presentations and other activities in professional associations and regional events, such as those sponsored by the Michigan Academy of Science, Arts and Letters. We also advocate for scholarship among students. We offer an honors program, and both undergraduate and graduate students are invited to participate in research symposia. Student participation in professional associations is also encouraged.

Fundamental to our community, however, is the spiritual component. We require all employees to assert agreement with our statement of faith (in the appendix below). This is not a bureaucratic matter. Rather, it is a confirmation that our most true community is our unity in Christ. As Christians, we know ourselves to be brothers and sisters at the most profound level, and we seek to express that reality in all our interactions in our community. Although we do not require all students to affirm our statement of faith, most of our students do affirm a personal relationship with Jesus Christ. Our instructional and cocurricular activities are all designed for Christians and to encourage our students' continued growth in Christ. It is our hope and indeed our consistent effort to demonstrate to our students what it means to be Christians individually and collectively. As a Christian higher educational institution, it is arguably our Christian community that is meant first and foremost in the first plank of The Concept. It is on that understanding that we have adopted a Community Covenant (attached below) setting forth our community behavioral expectations, even for those students who do not affirm our statement of faith.

Why is community important among faculty and staff and students? On a purely human level, we seek community and belonging. This is no less the case for adults than for young people, for faculty and staff than for students. This is a greater priority for a Christian university for at least two reasons.

The first is that as Christians, we are united in Christ. It has pleased God to call His people into fellowship with one another. Given our requirement that all faculty and staff be convinced Christians, we should be in community if not in communion with each other. We do not require that our students be Christians, although we do have behavioral standards that apply to all. But our employee community should be such that students can observe Christian fellowship in action.

The second reason that community is important in a Christian institution is our purpose to grow in our understanding of God. It is a commonplace to say that "all truth is God's truth." And, of course, this is true. But the driver of interdisciplinary collaboration and conversation is the "interdisciplinary" nature of God. The Triune God is inherently multifaceted but unified. He reveals Himself to us in all that He has created and engaged and sustained. Therefore, in every discipline, we examine some facet of God's self-revelation, whether in the physical world, in human and social studies, or in our God-endowed creative expression. In the same way in societal and vocational arenas, Christians experience different aspects of God's providence and guidance. However, as in the classic story of the blind men and the elephant, if we do not bring together our discoveries and insights, we will have only a partial if not an inaccurate understanding of God.

It is for this reason that we are a university. A university has been commonly understood as an educational institution that grants degrees of various levels through multiple schools focusing on cognate disciplines. As contemporary educational philosophy has lost its understanding of truth as united and coherent, more and more educational thinkers have preferred the term "multiversity" to reflect the diversities of studies undertaking within a single institution. A multiversity does not reflect or anticipate a unification of knowledge or pursuit of a single ultimate goal, such as understanding, worship, and enjoyment of God. Indeed, modern research and specialty- oriented universities almost militate against asking the big questions of origin, values, purpose, and destiny. Or each discipline crafts its own would-be grand answers, which are inevitably incomplete and inadequate for genuine human flourishing.

Some have argued that the first step toward a multiversity was the establishment of faculties and departments of theology, suggesting that theology was not a consideration of importance to all faculties and departments. Spring Arbor does have a department of theology, which supports both our Bible and theology course requirements for all students and majors for those seeking ministerial vocations. Nonetheless, we seek a pervasive biblical and theological perspective in all areas and so will remain an intentional and deliberate Christian university.

LEARNERS

Spring Arbor University, like all Christian persons and institutions, exists for God's glory. Our specific calling and purpose are to educate for Christ and His kingdom. Clearly, this entails a fundamental focus on those being educated: our learners. While we look to our faculty as learners to continue to pursue excellence and mastery in their academic disciplines, we obviously prioritize those who come to us for their education. And we ensure that all those who do come know that they will receive an intentionally thorough and pervasive Christian education.

Those learners and their requirements have changed since the writing of The Concept. Sixty years ago, Spring Arbor College offered undergraduate majors to residential or neighborhood students, usually of the "traditional" ages of roughly 17 to 22 years old. While we continue to cherish and serve traditional campus-based undergraduates, Spring Arbor University also cherishes and serves off-campus students of varying ages. Our academic offerings are no longer limited to bachelor's degrees. In addition to multiple master's degrees, we now grant the Doctor of Nursing Practice. Through such credentials as endorsements, certificates, and continuing education credits as well as degrees, we meet our learners' specific needs. As of 2023, the majority of our students are enrolled in graduate programs delivered remotely, by internet or Zoom. Our intent remains to provide to our students a Christian education in whatever format, medium, or credential best meets their needs. The academic content of that intent will be discussed later, but a key component of our education is personal and spiritual.

Scripture tells us that human beings are made in the image of God. That is our fundamental identity. We come to understand more of what that means as we come more to understand God Himself. In our society today, however, a multiplicity of possible identities is proposed, often based on the incomplete understandings of truth described above with respect to multiversities. Higher education institutions promulgating these understandings have had indirect but great influence on popular worldviews. Americans now seek their identity in physical attributes such as race or sexuality, social attributes such as political affiliations or loyalty to sports teams, or economic attributes such as profession or wealth, and so forth, with no overarching basis for evaluating each of these identities. One of the most important lessons we can teach our learners is their spiritual identity as having been intentionally and individually created in the image of God and as sufficiently robust to incorporate and support all their varied associations and distinctives.

To be sure, there is much discussion as to the meaning of the phrase "in the image of God." It does not mean a lack of diversity, as discussed above. Each human being images certain aspects of God. No human being other than Jesus is or ever has been the full image of God, and even Jesus emptied Himself of certain prerogatives of deity while on earth. This is at least one reason that all Christians together are the body of Christ rather than each one of us individually assuming that comprehensive identity. Again, this is why community is so important for Christians.

But to be in the image of God does mean that we are intended to reflect God's character and nature in this world. God has been pleased to reveal his character and nature not only generally in what He has created but specifically in His special revelation, the Bible. Therefore, if we seek to understand and embrace our true identity, we need to understand and embrace what God has revealed rather than the limited "revelations" of scholars, politicians, celebrities, and other societal influencers. Some have described this as a liberation, a freeing being squeezed into the most current, socially acceptable mold, to achieve one's true uniqueness. Spring Arbor University seeks to assist our learners to be grounded in their identity as being in the image of God, and by God's grace, in Christ.

We seek to accomplish this as Jesus did in His interactions with those he met. For those not adamantly and permanently opposed to Him, he expressed love, compassion, caring, and individual interest as well as patiently providing truth. Even with those who oppose the Gospel we offer, we remember that our struggle is not with flesh and blood, and that anyone with whom we interact may yet come to faith.

Further, in the last few years, we have received learners deeply affected by the dislocations in our society. These range from increasing numbers of broken homes, influences of the partial and malignant worldview denigrating their full humanity and significance, and the education disruption of the Covid-19 pandemic. The result has been students with significant struggles with mental health issues and a deep need to belong.

Therefore, we seek first to serve our learners as valuable persons who are welcome members of the Spring Arbor community. Our Student Development and Learning function strives to offer each student opportunities to:

- Grow in their faith in Jesus Christ
- Thrive in intellectual development
- Gain consistency between personal beliefs and behavior
- Accept responsibility as a member of the community
- Strengthen skills to manage life changes
- Flourish in a culturally diverse society

Advisors assist students in determining the courses and curricula to accomplish their goals. Faculty engage students in academics and in career and personal guidance. Instructional designers seek to provide user-friendly online and Zoom course access. Dormitory staff provide safe, comfortable housing. Business office and financial aid staff assist students in navigating college payments and funding. Student government offers a broad array of activities and entertainments as well as opportunities for community service. Student worker supervisors provide encouragement and examples of all good work as Christian vocation.

Spiritual Life Advisors assist student Bible study and prayer groups.

Beyond providing opportunities to belong, our staff and faculty play an important role in modeling Christian professionalism for our students. That modeling begins with the initiation of our admissions efforts and extends through our registrar's office completion of graduation documentation. Timely, accurate, and kindly assistance, particularly in areas where students are likely to have concerns such as in financial aid and billing operations, has a direct impact and provides opportunity for Christian service.

For a significant and increasing number of our campus students, athletics plays an important part in their Spring Arbor experience. Spring Arbor University Athletics' goals are representative of those of all our cocurricular activities. Its mission is to use the pursuit of athletic excellence to develop within our students depth of faith, strength of character, and skills of leadership essential for a lifetime of service to Jesus Christ. Participation in sports has been shown to contribute to holistic development of participants, and we value athletics as a venue for character formation. We want our athletes to experience personally the love of Christ and to express that love to teammates, opponents, and the community.

Lifelong Involvement in the Study and Application of the Liberal Arts

Lifelong

Anyone who has lived several decades recognizes that learning continues throughout life. Indeed, life has a way of teaching us unexpected lessons in unexpected ways. We frequently experience the need to learn new things, because we and our interests have changed or because the world has presented us with new circumstances. In Scripture, the Christian life is described as a walk, an extended exposure to new experiences. Further, our sanctification – becoming more like Christ – is described as a lifelong progression. Therefore, Spring Arbor University encourages our community to be intentional in our involvement in lifelong learning.

To ensure the efficacy of the education provided to our students, Spring Arbor University undertakes to support the continued scholarly and professional activities of our faculty. From the perspective of any learner, there is a particular delight that is available only as we grasp something new about an area with which we are already somewhat familiar. The language student discovers the literature and culture of another society as linguistic facility improves. The scientist explores ever more deeply seemingly familiar phenomena and so encounters ever greater complexity, wonder, and utility. The teacher finds a better way to convey a concept to a student. The historian uncovers evidence clarifying the motivation of a major figure's societal program and influence. The musician encounters melodic ornamentation versus reliance on chords and incorporates that approach in compositions. The engineer designs a long-sought solution by combining existing applications. Every arena offers such opportunities.

Our students and graduates face a society that is experiencing increasingly rapid changes in professional requirements. Societal forecasters now claim that today's college graduate should anticipate up to seven distinctive careers – not just jobs, but careers – during a working lifetime. Spring Arbor is committed to preparing our students to participate significantly in their careers and their transitions going forward. We accomplish this in the first instance through thorough presentation of the current state of each discipline in our established undergraduate and graduate programs. Further, we continue to develop new kinds of instructional delivery to meet the needs of more and more students. Such innovations are integral to our history.

Spring Arbor was founded to meet the educational needs of Free Methodists on what was then the frontier. We expanded from a "seminary" (initially elementary, then including a high school) to a junior college to a four-year college to a university and now to a doctoral granting institution. Along the way, we were among the very first Michigan higher education providers to meet the needs of prisoners and of adult degree-completion candidates through a network of physical locations all over the state. We launched online courses leading to fully online degrees early in the 21st century, and were well prepared for the online, Zoom, and hybrid offerings necessitated by the Covid-19 pandemic. We have offered continuing education units for teachers, post-masters certificates in nursing, accelerated teaching qualifications, non-degree social work courses, and numerous endorsements among other curricular innovations. We have partnered with specialists to provide distinctive degree options such as our Master's of Education in Trauma, which incorporates the international recognized curricula of Starr Commonwealth. And we seek to incorporate industry credential preparation in our coursework, such as teaching all the courses required for students to sit for the Certified Financial Planning credential examination.

Moreover, we value those whose callings are not necessarily to the professions. These include, for example, parents who choose to invest in their families rather than in their careers. In particular, those who homeschool their children experience the need for lifelong learning as they instruct their children. Spring Arbor University seeks to collaborate with those undertaking such efforts however we may be helpful.

In short, Spring Arbor is committed to ensuring that our faculty are lifelong learners within their disciplines, and that we offer appropriate vehicles for their continued professional and personal advancement to our current and potential students.

STUDY AND APPLICATION

The liberal arts are explicitly and implicitly inherent in all Spring Arbor University academic programs. The liberal arts are foundational to basic knowledge, habits of mind, and sheer enjoyment of the many arenas of life. How we regard the liberal arts themselves will be further discussed below, but in recent years there has been a tendency in academe to question the role of those studies in favor of more professional or vocational majors. Our position is that the liberal arts are foundational to those studies, and that professional or vocational programs are specific applications of the liberal arts rather than a truly separate category.

Particularly for our undergraduate students, our Core or general education program requires students to study the liberal arts disciplines at least on an introductory level and to pursue somewhat greater familiarity in one or two specific areas of study. At a bare minimum, every student is introduced to these basics of each discipline:

- Scope: What does this discipline seek to understand?

- Terms of Discourse: What are the basic ideas and vocabulary necessary to an informed investigation of issues that arise within this discipline?
- Means of Analysis: How does this discipline approach evaluating and identifying claims of truth, beauty, or virtue within its scope?
- Significance: What do the findings of this discipline contribute to human flourishing, and how do they display God's attributes, activity, and glory?

Interdisciplinary opportunities, such as our annual FOCUS days that bring together many faculty perspectives to address a single topic, encourage our students to develop and identify unexpected relationships that lead to creative thinking. Professional majors such as business, education, engineering, or nursing build directly on such liberal arts as history, economics, English, fine arts, communications, mathematics, physics, and biology. Spring Arbor's graduate programs emphasize and draw upon the underlying disciplines as well.

Even our "applied" colleagues such as our business faculty enjoy making the case for the liberal arts at their core. Here are faculty comments from a recent School of Business conversation on the liberal arts:

> "In business, we use all areas of liberal arts. Students don't just get the liberal arts (Gen Ed) behind them in order to take business courses.

The former will inform and equip students to look at their discipline, should I say, more holistically (thus avoiding tunnel vision); and as they work (which requires critical thinking skills) with other people who had different background/training, there will be increased harmony as each individual is capable of understanding and communicating with the other people more effectively.

The liberal arts are foundational to being a well-versed and knowledgeable human being with a broad worldview. The liberal arts includes logic and reasoning, knowledge acquisition in diverse fields, creative thinking, problem solving, communication skills, which are, in essence, soft skills that are sought by most employers today. It means that we take something from each area of human development and include that in the students' well-rounded education. We need to view each area of study not just from our discipline, but through the lens of the liberal arts."

And our social work faculty commit to:

"Incorporate content in social work courses that ties back to the general education courses our student have taken. When we tie back to the general education requirements, they understand how it all ties together and equips them to be competent social workers. It is going from theory to practice."

Employers have increasingly recognized and valued what are termed "soft skills." Such skill development is clearly a focus of Spring Arbor's liberal arts courses and serves as a starting point from which to discuss how the general education program at SAU connects with the development of skills and characteristics identified for success in the professional arena. Employers commonly express the desire for college graduates to have strong skills in written and oral communication, critical thinking, problem-solving, adaptability, and collaboration. These are exactly the skills that students develop when given a broad liberal arts education. Analytical skills and attention to detail grow through practice with mathematics, the scientific method, and attentive reading, listening, and observation. Practice in these areas creates new neural pathways that increase the ability to learn, understand increasingly complex ideas, and make connections between unlikely areas. Understanding complexity and nuance grows empathy and humility. Exposure to the diversity of human experience and cultures increases adaptability and enhances interpersonal skills. Through a broad foundation of learning, these various skills are connected and reinforced. In addition, study of the liberal arts also provides practice with higher level soft skills, such as collaboration. As confidence grows regarding the ability to learn, think, and communicate effectively, leadership skills grow as well.

Moreover, as a Christian university, we emphasize application of theological and spiritual disciplines, both in academics and in cocurricular offerings. Inclusion of biblical study and spiritual disciplines develop the Fruit of the Spirit – love, joy, peace, patience, kindness, goodness, faithfulness, gentleness, and self-control (Galatians 5:22-23) – and reinforce character attributes such as responsibility, integrity, empathy, collaboration, future orientation, and conflict resolution.

As the internet, social media, and other resources provide more and more of the strictly informational content that used to come from attending educational institutions, and as artificial intelligence comes increasingly able to replicate traditional "thinking" and "writing" tasks, society needs not only critical thinking to evaluate the flood of information but also to develop that judgment and discretion that is distinctly human. This is also known as wisdom, the skill of living well, of making best use of resources available, including informational resources and new technologies that might modify or even replace traditionally human tasks. Spring Arbor University affirms that even or perhaps especially in these matters, "The fear of the Lord is the beginning of wisdom: and the knowledge of the Holy One is understanding" (Proverbs 9:10). We see this as one of the distinctive and highly applicable advantages of Christian higher education.

LIBERAL ARTS

Spring Arbor University is committed to Jesus Christ as Savior and Lord, and as the perspective for learning. The University exists to educate for Christ and His kingdom. SAU utilizes the broad approach and perspective of a liberal arts education, involving the pursuit of all truth as God's truth, as the mechanism to develop the intellect and Christian character in all students. Also inherent in our educational approach is the commitment to the value and potential of every human being as created in God's image and responsible for effective, redemptive participation in society and culture. We desire to prepare our students to "always be prepared to give an answer to everyone who asks you to give the reason for the hope you have, and do this with gentleness and respect." (I Peter 3:15)

The traditional idea of a liberal education was exposure to the breadth of human learning. Having exposure to a broad foundation of academic disciplines is an integral part of our undertaking. Spring Arbor University's goal for all our students is to recognize the interconnectedness of all learning and its contribution to our knowledge of God. This goal goes well beyond the liberal arts, but it is an integral part of our undertaking.

Historically, the liberal arts were very specifically the skills that free ("Liber" in Latin) citizens of the classical world needed to have to participate in the decision-making processes of their cities. In short, decisions were shaped by the ability of the participants to persuade others of their viewpoint. For this reason, the earliest liberal arts were the three ways (tri-via or trivium) consisting of grammar, logic, and rhetoric. In short, even the very earliest of the liberal arts were, ironically, vocational. If one considers the focus of the activity, knowledge of society (sociology), history (to persuade by reference to the founders), and psychology also played key roles. So, in the earliest stages, the liberal arts involved aspects of what we now view as the humanities and the social sciences.

The remaining four elements of traditional liberal arts (the four ways, or quadrivium) derive from the philosophers known as the Pythagoreans. Their focus was on various ways of conceiving of mathematics. The first was mathematics itself, known as arithmetic. The second was mathematics in space, also known as geometry. The third was mathematics in time, or music. Finally, mathematics in space and time was astronomy. Looked at from a modern perspective, "arithmetic" could easily include computer science. "Geometry" could include the range of three-dimensional disciplines from architecture and sculpture to engineering.

"Astronomy" clearly stands as an example of observational science. Simply put, the liberal arts easily encompass a considerable portion of the breadth of human learning.

A critical outcome from a liberal arts education is that it teaches students how to learn in a variety of ways and through a variety of topics. The ability to learn new information is critical to long-term success. Developing a long-term appreciation for learning and the desire to continue to learn is an ideal outcome since it will serve graduates long after their initial college experience. Exposure to many areas of study builds confidence in one's ability to pursue learning in fields beyond one's initial major or degree.

Students who receive only vocationally focused training will be more limited in their ability to embrace new areas of learning. Today's graduates should anticipate multiple changes of career, the need to develop new skills within their career, the ability to learn new information, and the need to adapt as necessary to success. In short, the liberal arts can truly be seen as the "liberating arts," providing avenues for flexibility and choice. As employers begin to compete with traditional higher education by offering employment-specific training to their employees, the value of exposure to the breadth of learning as a foundation on which to build specific expertise may well become more obvious over time. Someone trained by an employer for that employer's needs may be less confident in learning new material not tied immediately to the employer.

As Spring Arbor pursues its goal of enabling its students to express in their individual ways the image of God and to become critical participants in the contemporary world, the freedom of mind to address new circumstances and challenges is an integral part of our liberal arts-grounded educational offerings. Even skilled tradesmen benefit from involvement in liberal arts, particularly as they may become business owners and employers. And, returning to the original purpose of the liberal arts, citizens in a democracy need skills of mind and action to play well their proper role in the society of which they are a part.

That said, Spring Arbor University views as the most liberating of the liberal arts a thorough knowledge of the Christian faith and Gospel. Recognition and understanding of the love, sovereignty, promises, and trustworthiness of God provide a foundation for life and action without equivalent in any other scheme of education. That is the basis of our total commitment to Jesus Christ as the perspective for learning.

Total Commitment to Jesus Christ as the Perspective for Learning

Total Commitment

Spring Arbor University is a Christian community. Some today regard religion as a personal, limited set of convictions. We prefer the original notion of the term "religion" from the Latin meaning aligning with reality. The fundamental reality with which we align our education is as revealed by the Bible: the Old and New Testaments.

In Genesis 1 we learn that all that came into existence was created by God. Scripture indicates that all was created to show forth the excellencies and attributes of God and further to accomplish his purpose to bring forth a people with whom to have a loving, intimate relationship. To this end, humankind was created in God's image, to a degree enjoying His communicable attributes so that humankind might both in some sense represent God to the rest of creation and enjoy a genuine relationship with the Creator.

This relationship did, however, require loyalty on the part of humankind to God, and a failure in that loyalty removed the possibility of the intimacy that was not only necessary to the relationship but also to sustained human life. The breach of trust was such that humans continue in rebellion and are unqualified to mend the situation. God Himself needed to rectify the situation, which He did through the Son, the second person of the Trinity.

Colossians 1 tells us that all things in heaven and on earth, visible and invisible, whether thrones or dominions or rulers or authorities, had been created by, through, and for the second person of the Son, who became incarnate as the man Jesus the Christ. Moreover, Jesus sustains all things, and in Him all things hold together. It is only in Him that the universal and personal purposes of creation are accomplished. This is the fundamental reality within which all existence take place. We regard any other view as deficient and inadequate as a perspective for learning, life, and society. Scripture advises that we who are mature in the faith – and we seek to ensure that all our administration, faculty, and staff are mature in the faith – are not to be blown to and fro by the shifting winds of societal opinion. God is unchanging; so also should be our commitment to Him and His self-revelation, particularly through God, the Son, the second Person of the Trinity, who took on human nature as Jesus, the Christ.

JESUS CHRIST

Scripture tells us that it pleased God to create as a means of expressing and displaying His attributes. He created humanity for His joy and glory. As set forth in President Ellis' *Grace and Truth,* the Bible does affirm that humankind was made by God in His image but also that, individually and collectively, human beings have rebelled against their sovereign creator, preferring their own opinions and priorities, and trusting in their own sufficiency and standards of goodness. This rebellion, also known as "sin," has created a breach between God and the entire human race. Although God has mercifully continued to exercise His benevolence toward his rebellious creatures, that breach inevitably has placed every person under a sentence of eternal separation from God, a separation evidenced by the reality of death in this world. Moreover, this breach has to some degree affected every aspect of human life, so that reliance on our own instincts and inclinations inevitably leads to personal and societal grief and evil.

God would have been thoroughly justified in eliminating humanity and the whole physical creation that had been affected by human sin. But, again, it pleased God to extend mercy to His creation and creatures and to devise a plan within the Trinity to reconcile the rebels to Himself in a way consistent with His justice and holiness. God the Son, as Jesus the Messiah, executed the plan to heal the breach between God and humankind by becoming and living as a human being the life of complete loyalty to God that a loving relationship requires. Human death is warranted and legitimate due to disloyalty, sinful self-reliance, and separation from God who sustains us. Death, however, had no right to Jesus, who was loyal and sinless, and who lived His life in dependence and communion with God. Yet He willingly suffered death in the place of those who trust in Him, and to them His righteousness is credited so that they are acceptable to and reconciled with God.

Christianity is unique among all the world's philosophies, religions, and worldviews. All other views anticipate some form of human self-improvement to the point of approval by fundamental reality, whether viewed as impersonal undifferentiated existence or personal deity. Only Christianity requires perfect righteousness, recognizes that human beings cannot attain such holiness, and provides the required perfection through trust in the saving intervention of God Himself in the person of Jesus the Christ, and the application of Jesus' righteousness to those who trust in Him.

The Perspective for Learning.

Every area of learning depends upon certain underlying assumptions. These are usually examined in the disciplines of "philosophy of" – the philosophy of science, the philosophy of history, etc. Underlying those philosophies are even more foundational concepts of reality and truth. The Christian understanding of all that exists as created, sustained, and revealed in Jesus Christ, the second person of the Triune God, provides those foundational concepts of reality and truth. This may sound very abstract but actually has very direct implications on the Spring Arbor approach to learning.

In the first instance, we regard truth as correspondence with the reality that God created and sustains in which we live and move and have our being. Moreover, all truths are part of a unified truth in God. That belief in unified truth underlies the idea of a university, an institution in which all truths are to be sought and examined to lead to a greater understanding of God Himself. The idea that all truth contributes to our knowledge of God further animates our commitment to broad exposure to the areas of learning for our students, not least because Jesus Christ declared Himself "the way, and the truth, and the life." (John 14:6).

As to our faculty, staff, and students, we recognize each person as made in the image of God, endowed with physical, intellectual, and moral capabilities, created and called for specific contributions in God's governance of the world. Therefore, we seek to contribute to the flowering of each student's individual gifting and abilities through comprehensive curricula, campus experience, and personalized guidance and support.

As to specific academic disciplines, according to Romans 1:20, God's "invisible attributes, namely his eternal power and divine nature, have been clearly perceived, ever since the creation of the world, in the things that have been made." (ESV). John's Gospel (1:1-3) discloses that Christ was the Word through whom the creation of the universe was accomplished. That creation provides both the resources with which, and the theater within which, human beings can express the image of God within them. Therefore, all our circumstances, creativity, and accomplishments take place within those parameters. Further, God has chosen to reveal Himself not only in the original creation but also in ongoing involvement in the world as recorded for our guidance in the Bible. These realities are the basis of the perspective we bring to life, learning and society – that is, Jesus Christ as *the* perspective for all these issues and circumstances. As but a single instance, our social work faculty believe Christ to have been the first social worker and seek to follow His example in their practice and to present His model to their students.

The Christian higher education agenda of the later 20th century and continuing into the 21st century is the integration of faith and learning. By "integration" it is meant the investigation and expression of the foundations of academic disciplines in God's actions and self-disclosure. Such integration includes consideration of the origin, purpose, values, and direction/destiny of the academic discipline. Forty years after The Concept became Spring Arbor's mission statement, our faculty wrote a series of essays, collected and published as The Concept books, setting forth such integration in a number of disciplines. These essays expressed and reinforced the dependence on human intellectual and cultural accomplishments on God's prior creation and continuing involvement in creation.

For example, all language arts arise because God endowed human beings with words and chose to communicate with us in words, not least of all in the Scriptures. The Bible speaks frequently of songs, and no other species composes music in anything resembling the range of human music. God reveals Himself in history, both by His appearance and through the direction of historical events. The sciences as we know them are possible because God has created and sustains consistent, discoverable laws governing natural processes.

Jesus Christ as the perspective for learning also affects our teaching. As a senior faculty member recently reflected: "Christ is the lens through which we see the world. He is the foundation of our worldview and in this context our discipline, whether it is biology, business, Spanish, nursing, math, theology, or anything in between. ... Christ is the reason and model of all we do. We teach ... a useful and God-honoring discipline that will allow us to serve others. ... Christ Himself is a teacher. ... While he didn't teach all disciplines, He modeled for us what it means to be a learner with a mission – to serve others through our God-given talents and skills."

These disclosures of God's attributes are not limited to the "academic" disciplines. The first person described in Scripture as filled by the Holy Ghost was an artisan. Scripture abounds in stories based in "practical" arts ranging from agriculture to politics. All are appropriate venues for exploration and exposure of God's image in each of us.

Recognition of the permeation of all these areas by God's truth is not something to be limited to the Christian academy. It needs to be shared prophetically with the needy world. This responsibility is arguably an integral part of our total commitment to Jesus Christ and our commitment to:

CRITICAL PARTICIPATION IN THE CONTEMPORARY WORLD

Although some previous generations of Christians have sought to preserve their witness by withdrawing from the world, Spring Arbor University takes seriously that Jesus does not ask that His followers be taken out of the world (John 17:15) but that we, through our good deeds and positive contributions to the contemporary world, might bring glory to God (Ephesians 2:10). By critical participation, we seek to be the salt and light that Christ calls us to be in the Gospel according to Matthew 5:13-14.

CRITICAL PARTICIPATION: LEARNERS

As an educational institution, Spring Arbor University exists to advance God's kingdom by preparing our graduates to assume positions of influence – not necessarily of title or prestige, but of genuine influence – through the excellence of their professional and personal contributions in each of their callings, and as well-prepared ambassadors for Christ. To that end, Spring Arbor's Academic Affairs, faculty, Marketing and Enrollment teams, and Career Development office seek to be aware of the expectations of prospective students and their families as well as their potential employers to ensure that we provide the academic, professional, and cocurricular programs and experiences to prepare our learners for their anticipated futures. As indicated earlier, we also seek to ensure that our students are in the best sense liberally educated so that they can continue to learn and contribute throughout their professional and personal lives.

Part of that preparation and a distinctive of Spring Arbor is our cross-cultural studies program for our undergraduates. In addition to such conventional and important opportunities as semesters abroad, we provide short-term travel under faculty guidance to countries, key features of whose cultures students have studied in the preceding semester as part of our Core or general education offerings. We first sent students around the world in 1985 with the intent that our students experience the light of God's love for humanity and the world. Recent trips have visited Bulgaria, Cambodia, Costa Rica, Guatemala, Nepal, Czech Republic, England, Scotland, and Israel.

Throughout, Spring Arbor provides opportunities to our learners to understand the Christian faith and, as the Holy Spirit enables, to come to faith, to be able to apply that worldview to their various callings, and to explain the Gospel to those they will encounter as they serve as critical participants in the world. Current students are challenged by social and intellectual currents such as "the new atheism," which questions the very existence of God, or "moralistic, therapeutic deism," which claims that the creator exists but is not involved in our lives other than to expect us to be "good" and to help us with our problems. We seek to prepare our students to address currents such as these, issues arising from the increasing presence of other faiths in our country, and attempts by cults to become more mainstream by claiming to be Christian. The best preparation to be a critical participant in the spiritual needs of those our students will encounter is a thorough preparation in the foundations of the Gospel of Jesus Christ provided in the holy scriptures. We seek to provide that to all our Spring Arbor University students.

Although we have done our best to contribute to the development of our learners and alumni, we are humbled by their accomplishments in the contemporary world, both as professionals working from a Christian worldview and as sharers of the Good News of reconciliation with God through Jesus Christ.

CRITICAL PARTICIPATION: SPRING ARBOR UNIVERSITY

Spring Arbor University strives to be known for its integrity, whether in its communication with students, its participation in the broader community, or its financial dealings. Just as our alumni earn credibility to discuss the biblical perspectives with colleagues, Spring Arbor itself must have standing among those with whom we communicate to gain a hearing for the Christian worldview. This is particularly the case since we find ourselves in an era of either disinterest or active mistrust of the Christian faith.

Much as our fundamental purpose is to educate for Christ and His kingdom from a biblical perspective for learning, life, and society, we recognize a related responsibility for Christian higher education to enter into the national conversation with respect to how individuals and society should address contemporary issues.

In the mid-20th century, particularly in the wake of what was termed "the Eisenhower revival," it was reasonably accurate to assume at least broad societal exposure to some of the ideas of Christianity. That is no longer the case. Surveys by Barna, Pew, and other groups indicate an ever-decreasing understanding of essential teachings of Christianity, in some cases even among apparent evangelical Christians.

This has come about in part due to the 30-plus-year effort of the homosexual community, as initially set forth in Kirk and Madsen's "After the Ball," to paint Christians as oppressors of innocents. There was also a steady stream of writings during the independence movements in Africa and Asia to position missionaries as agents of colonial oppression particularly in destruction of indigenous cultures. And Critical Race Theory has popularized the idea that inequality of outcomes, known as inequity, is due to oppression, including by Christians.

Most importantly, however, secular institutions of higher education have promulgated and popularized versions of enlightenment skepticism and post-modern rejection of universal truth resulting in the rejection of any claim of a comprehensive, universal explanation of origin, purpose, values, or destiny. During this time, Christian higher education, while actively engaged in integration of faith and knowledge as well as producing well-regarded scholars within various disciplines, has not successfully engaged this intellectual assault on universal truth by articulating the Christian worldview outside of the Christian community. Even today, books by Christians addressing "wokeness" and other worldview concerns tend to be more addressed to how Christians can protect themselves from such ideas rather than engaging these alternative worldviews in the broader social conversation. It is ironic that prominent and successful contemporary challengers of the prevailing metanarratives – such as Jordan Peterson, Dennis Prager, and Ben Shapiro – are not Christians.

Spring Arbor University as an institution seeks to be a critical participant in the contemporary world. Clearly, our primary opportunity for such participation is in educating our students from a profoundly Christian perspective and sending them out prepared to engage the arenas to which they are called with both professional excellence and readiness to present the claims of Christ. However, we also clearly see the responsibility of Christian higher education to set forth the biblical worldview as the alternative to the malign worldviews currently in ascendence and to do so prophetically, wisely, and winsomely, seeking God's enablement to influence this contemporary world utterly lost without recognizing the call of God upon each person's life. The 21st-century challenges that we foresee at this point and our institutional commitments considering those challenges are set after discussion of how Spring Arbor has implemented the planks of The Concept.

THE CONCEPT IN ACTION

Spring Arbor University is a community of learners distinguished by our lifelong involvement in the study and application of the liberal arts, total commitment to Jesus Christ as the perspective for learning, and critical participation in the contemporary world.

What, then, have been the results of The Concept? To answer this fully is not possible in short course, but here are some specific institutional activities that seek to implement the planks of The Concept and some brief vignettes of how The Concept has influenced students, alumni, faculty, and friends of Spring Arbor.

Spring Arbor University is a Community of Learners

Although achievement of community is the responsibility of every constituency of Spring Arbor University, the institutional charge falls most directly on our Office of Student Development and Success. The Department seeks to meet the spiritual, social, intellectual, and emotional needs of our students. Living in the Spring Arbor University community will offer each student opportunities to:

- Grow in their faith in Jesus Christ
- Thrive in intellectual development
- Gain consistency between personal beliefs and behavior
- Accept responsibility as a member of the community
- Strengthen skills to manage life changes
- Flourish in a culturally diverse society

The Department focuses on advising and other services to support student success in completion of academic goals, particularly degrees and credentials. The overall approach includes:

ELIMINATING BARRIERS
>Reform administrative policies
>Leverage microgrant program
>Simplify early academic planning

Proactively manage advising caseloads

Develop pre-college academic and
psychosocial preparation program

Formalize student success leadership

ENHANCING SUPPORT AND MOTIVATION

Case management system for supporting students

Coordinate student support networks

Foster social support and personal belongingness

Develop and manage 4-year academic plans

Encourage pedagogical development of instructors

ENRICHING VALUE

Redesign supplemental milestone courses

Streamline prerequisite and program requirement
pathways

Embed experiential learning in the curriculum

Strategically sequence career guidance and
exploration in courses

Spring Arbor's extracurricular experiences are designed to shape students just as much as their studies. Applying classroom learning, serving peers in student leadership positions, and connecting with others in our clubs and student organizations are important aspects of our community. With more than 50 clubs, activities, organizations, and ministry opportunities, Spring Arbor has something for everyone!

Examples of Academic Activities:

Enactus: The Enactus team is a group of students of diverse backgrounds, majors, and experiences who come together to locate needs in the community and develop creative ways of meeting those needs. We do not look to just "give" people fish, but instead we pride ourselves on "teaching" people to fish and creating sustainable projects economically, environmentally, and socially. We then compile these projects and present them before CEOs and Presidents of globally known and recognized Fortune 500 companies.

Epsilon Chi: It is the intention of Epsilon Chi to connect the education students on campus with the community around them as well as the one they reside in. This means creating opportunities with principals, administrators, schools, teachers, professors, and other education majors on campus.

Model Arab League: Model Arab League is an event sponsored through the National Council on U.S.-Arab Relations in which students learn about the politics and history of the Arab world as they study a particular Arab nation and then prepare to "represent" that nation at a mock Arab League summit. Every year, SAU sends a team to the Model Arab League convention held at a participating Michigan university.

Multicultural and Intercultural Student Organizations: Students of all colors and backgrounds are celebrated and supported on Spring Arbor University's campus. With more than 10 organizations dedicated to fostering a dialogue between various ethnicities and promoting multiculturalism on SAU's campus, there is something for everyone.

Social Etiquette Dinner: As students look to graduation, they are invited in February to participate in the Social Etiquette Dinner, where an expert leads students through a formal dinner, instructing them on the dos and don'ts of dining in a professional setting. This is a service offered through the Career Services office.

Social Work Association: This group is open to all social work majors and those expressing an interest in social work as a major. Social work majors elect cabinet members and have total control and responsibility for programming within the guidelines for student organizations at Spring Arbor University. The goals that this organization established for itself are:

- Create a greater awareness of the community and the community's needs.
- Inform students to create new resources if current resources do not exist or fail to meet the needs of the community.
- Give students an opportunity to interact with other students in their major.

- Motivate students to become involved in some form of social work.

Undergraduate Research Symposium: Each spring, Spring Arbor hosts a symposium where students can present their research to their peers and professors. The symposium is run similarly to an academic conference: there are concurrent sessions of three or four presenters with time for questions at the end of each panel. In addition, the top three essays receive cash prizes.

ART, MUSIC, MEDIA, LITERATURE ACTIVITIES

Art Shows: Every fall and spring, senior art majors are given the chance to showcase their most awe-inspiring artistic endeavors in the Ganton Art Gallery.

Chapel Band: The Chapel Band performs at the beginning of almost every chapel service, leading the students, faculty, and staff into a time of worship to the Lord. The Chapel Band encourages students of a variety of musical backgrounds to try out for this exciting and crucial part of each chapel service.

Gospel Choir: This choir brings together a diverse set of singers and musicians to clap, shout, and sing their praises to God. The group performs for area churches and prisons, and every year organizes a Gospel Fest, which is an eclectic performance featuring a wide variety of talent.

Jazz Band: All of Spring Arbor's instrumental musicians are encouraged to try out for the Jazz Band, which performs concerts throughout the year and organizes the annual Jazz Bash.

Musical Ensembles: Those gifted with musical ability are welcome to try out for a variety of musical ensembles, including: Chamber Singers, Concert Band, Concert Choir, and Wellspring. These groups perform throughout the year and tour around the country.

Radio Stations: SAU Radio broadcasts from Sayre Decan Hall on campus, while 106.9 HOME.fm is a professionally staffed commercial radio station airing throughout south-central Michigan that trains student broadcasters throughout the day, playing "Music that Makes You Feel Good." The Message is an online Christian radio station where students interested in radio can get their start. Students volunteer as they learn alongside professionals on the air.

SAU Hearts Drama: From dazzling musicals to cutting-edge black-box theater performances to award-winning plays, the Spring Arbor theater program offers a wide range of theatrical outlets to sate the appetite of the most enthusiastic theater guru.

Will Shoot for Credit: This is a semester-long course that focuses on short film production. Anyone is welcome to come to the class to learn more about production. Students pitch short film ideas, and four of them are chosen to produce. Auditions for actors, script readings with the cast, storyboards, and props are done outside of class before the scheduled production date. The director works with the editor to finalize the short film, which is screened at the Will Shoot for Credit event.

The G.K. Chesterton Society: This reading group meets once a month to discuss Chesterton's plays, poems, novels, essays, and criticism. In good Chestertonian spirit, their meetings are full of laughter, appreciation, cheese, and cookies. They welcome anyone who wants to follow Chesterton in thinking, living, and loving with gusto and gratitude.

The Oak Tree Review: This is Spring Arbor's literary journal. It publishes the creative works of students, including poetry, fiction, nonfiction, scripts, and reviews. Students also serve as editors and oversee the publication process. In the fall, *The Oak Tree Review* sponsors a poetry reading where students and faculty share their latest work, and each spring there is a journal release party where students read from the latest issue.

Tolkien Literary Club: This club's main purpose is to enjoy, learn from, and gain a greater appreciation of the works of J.R.R. Tolkien. Meetings focus on reading books and other literature penned by him. Reading is regularly accompanied with insights about the passage and an increased knowledge of the context. Meetings are welcome to all, both the seasoned Tolkien veterans and those who have not yet been initiated.

Writing Center: The Writing Center exists to help members of the SAU community grow as writers. It offers space for students to learn in community by engaging in conversations about all aspects of writing and critical thinking. Many of the tutors who work here are English majors. Working with others' writing is an excellent way to hone your own craft.

TRADITIONAL FUN FOR ALL ANNUAL EVENTS

80s Skate Night: Grab your tracksuits, your fluorescent leg warmers, and your distressed denim jackets! SAU reserves the roller rink for one crazy and colorful night for you to turn back the clock and have some '80s-style fun.

Arbor Games: Think the Olympics, throw in some silly games, some tests of endurance, strength, and coordination, complete with fun costumes and unpredictable team skits, and you've got a glimpse of this popular annual event.

Block Party: It's everything you'd want from an end-of-the-summer block party, minus your mom's potato salad. Campus members play sports, participate in fun games, grill some hot dogs, and just enjoy being together.

Choptoberfest: So, you think you can saw? Prove it at Choptoberfest! Participate in an assortment of lumberjack and highlander games where it's survival of the fittest. The event is hosted by the Ogle Villages.

Feminar: No boys allowed! This is a girls-ONLY night where Holton Health Center staff facilitate discussions about health, relationships, and spirituality ... with a side of chocolate.

Late-Night Breakfast: Finals got you down? Not anymore. On the night before the start of final exam week, the SAU faculty and staff serve up breakfast and deliver their own entertainment for the sleep-deprived and energy-deficient students.

Lip Sync: You can't miss this night of wacky performances in the spring. It's karaoke at the next level. Students, and sometimes staff or faculty, practice for weeks to put on the greatest musically dubbed performance of the year.

Lowell's Last Dance: Put on your dancing shoes at this annual Lowell Hall event. There is dancing on the basketball court, karaoke, snacks, volleyball, and more!

Mystery Date Night: Hoping to spend some time with that special someone, but you don't know who that special someone is?! Look no further than Andrews Hall Mystery Date Night! Let our warm and friendly event heat up your icy cold November heart with fun laughs and free hot cocoa! What are the chances you'll meet your future spouse? Well, it's definitely not guaranteed, but you will at least have a good time.

Porchfest: The most highly anticipated event of the year, this SNL-format variety show brings together the most (and least) talented people that SAU has to offer. One of the longest-running and most historic traditions on campus, this is one event you will remember for years to come.

Salon Des Refuses: All dressed up and no place to go? Come on over to Andrews Hall for the art show of the ages. Often featuring artwork by Jonathan Rinck, the show is primarily a collection of work created by SAU art students. It's a celebration of the time and effort the students put into preparing for the many wonderful art shows put on by the art department here.

FITNESS AND ATHLETICS

Spring Arbor recognizes that we are physical beings, as well as intellectual and spiritual. For a significant number of our campus students, athletics plays an important part in their Spring Arbor experience. Spring Arbor University Athletics seeks to use the pursuit of athletic excellence to develop within our student-athletes a depth of faith, strength of character, and skills of leadership essential for a lifetime of service to Jesus Christ. Our core values in athletics are representative of the comprehensive mission of every component of our institution. Among them, our goal is to develop young men and women who love God with all their heart, soul, mind, and strength, and who love neighbors as themselves. Sports tend to foster individualism; we will commit to serving others, including our community and our opponents. We want our athletes to recognize that their talents are a gift from God to be used for His glory.

Our athletic resources include six facilities located on campus: the McDonald Athletic Center (basketball, volleyball), Hank Burbridge Field (baseball), Cougar Softball Field, the Cougar Soccer Complex, Jones Tennis Complex, and the Ralph G. Walker Memorial Track. There are two fitness centers located inside the McDonald Athletic Center, one for athletic teams and the other, the Faith Small Fitness Center, open to all for weightlifting, aerobic exercise, yoga, and rehabilitation. The golf and bowling teams have off-campus facilities for competition and practice, both located in Jackson, Michigan, less than 20 minutes from campus.

Our intercollegiate athletic teams compete regionally in the Crossroads League (crossroadsleague.com) and nationally in the National Association of Intercollegiate Athletics (naia.org). Men's teams are available in baseball, basketball, bowling, cross country, golf, soccer, tennis, and track and field. Women's sports are basketball, bowling, cross country, golf, soccer, softball, tennis, track and field, and volleyball. We also offer coed competitive cheer. While we seek success for our sports teams in the form of winning competitions and championships, we value athletics as a venue for character formation. Participation in sports has been shown to contribute to holistic development of participants. Although our men's basketball and women's soccer teams have won national championships, Spring Arbor University is particularly proud of our teams' records as National Association of Intercollegiate Athletics (NAIA) Five Star Champions of Character as well as Scholar Teams for many years running.

Intramural sports allow students to engage in physical fitness through sports without the formality of intercollegiate competition. Commonly offered are these intramural leagues for men and women:

- Basketball
- Beach Volleyball
- Flag Football
- Floor Hockey
- Indoor Soccer
- Indoor Volleyball
- Outdoor Soccer
- Ultimate Frisbee

SPRING ARBOR COMMUNITY BUILDERS

Faculty: The Lowells

During the Great Depression, faculty were often unpaid, and some, including LeRoy M. Lowell, formally relinquished claims to portions of back pay "if and when settlement is paid in full for the balance due for services rendered." Despite this, Mrs. Lowell made certain that the students were not neglected. She was famous for her chocolate peanut cookies regularly provided to students also affected by Depression realities. Here is her recipe, preserved by Edith Spencer, class of 1935, one of the earliest "nontraditional' age students:

2 cups sugar, 1 cup shortening, ¾ cup cocoa, 1 egg, (salt) or salted peanuts, 1 cup sour milk, 1 teaspoon soda, vanilla, 3 cups flour … "to drop"

Dr. Lowell later served as President of Spring Arbor from 1935 to 1944 and again from 1955 to 1957. During his first tenure, he was able to liquidate the last of the accumulated debt from the Depression years.

Trustee: Hugh White, Class of 1923

After leaving Spring Arbor Seminary, Dr. Hugh White studied at Western Michigan and the University of Michigan. He was named to the Spring Arbor Board of Trustees in 1932. At that time, a concern in Chicago that sold groceries to the school needed funds for its own bills and so was foreclosing on the campus. Dr. White, at the time a CPA in what became the firm of White, Bower and Prevo, personally assumed the debt so that the money would not be taken from the school. He was assisted in this effort by Rev. William Lloyd Stephenson, who had come to Spring Arbor for ministerial training in 1912 and whose son and grandson subsequently served as trustees. Monies were raised over the next two years from the Alumni League and other donors, including Dr. White, to the point where the debt could be carried again by the school. In 1957, Dr. White became Chairman of the Board of Trustees and served in that capacity for the next 28 years, after which he was succeeded on the Board by his son Glenn, who served from 1962 to 1998, and his grandson, David, who served from 1986 until 2022.

Campus Student: Judith Colson Ganton, Spring Arbor High School Class of 1960

Despite her family being Roberts Wesleyan loyalists, Judi decided at 10 years of age to attend Spring Arbor and to get her name on a rock, indicating she had become a Class Officer. She was allowed to go to Spring Arbor because Roberts Wesleyan had closed their high school. She remembers fondly a series of machinations that made her, though new to the school and not a "townie," to be elected to class office and to achieve her dream of her name on the rock at her graduation. Although she completed nursing school elsewhere, Judi and her husband Lloyd, owners of Lloyd Ganton Retirement Centers, remain deeply involved in Spring Arbor, from Judi's leading the alumni association, to both selected as Alumnus of the Year, to both serving on the Board and becoming Life Trustees ... with their names on more than a rock. Judi recalls, "I am so thankful for the chapels where I cemented my faith in Christ, for the parents that probably sacrificed to send me there, and two alums, Pastors James Mannoia and Robert Canfield, that took the time to encourage a teenager to go to a Christian school. ...

I love it and will continue to do everything that I can for the school."

Friends of Spring Arbor: E Harold Munn, Media Executive

Harold Munn was not a graduate of Spring Arbor but served as a Trustee for 50 years from 1960 to 2010. He was the impetus behind Spring Arbor's entry into radio broadcasting and an advocate of student involvement in the media. Since childhood, Hal was a member of the Free Methodist Church and served that denomination in many volunteer administrative capacities from 1950 to 2015. He received his Federal Communications Commission (FCC) radio license at age 14 and in 1947, at age 17, became a lifetime member of the Institute of Electrical and Electronic Engineers (IEEE), the world's largest professional organization of any scientific profession. The following year he graduated from Hillsdale College. He taught high school for two years before starting his first radio stations in Coldwater, Michigan. In addition to radio, he was a pioneer in broadband communications, received one of the three first cable TV permits awarded by the FCC, and started many cable companies, including Coldwater and Columbia Cablevision. In 1950, Hal established the E. Harold Munn, Jr. and Associates broadcast engineering consulting firm in Coldwater, and in that capacity built or consulted with about 800 radio stations in all 50 states and on nearly 70 colleges and university campuses.

Lifelong Involvement in the Study and Application of the Liberal Arts

The purpose of Spring Arbor University is to educate for Christ and His kingdom from a biblical perspective for learning, life, and society. The General Education curriculum in SAU's undergraduate programs grows out of the SAU Concept. As followers of Christ who are committed to Christ as the perspective for learning, the University utilizes the study and application of the liberal arts to provide a broad foundation of knowledge on which academic disciplines can be built and develop from. The mixture of required general education courses provides breadth of perspective and various ways of knowing to promote transformational growth in the Christian faith while also developing the intellect and the ability to interact with others effectively.

As a Christian liberal arts institution, the University cares deeply about the Christian faith, the long history of God's revelation through the written word of Scripture, and the living word of Jesus Christ. The University believes the most distinctive and the most important of the liberal arts is the study of the Bible and theology to provide a thorough knowledge of the Christian faith and Gospel. This study, provided through a firmly Christian lens, is one of the highly applicable advantages of Christian higher education.

Recognition and understanding of the love, sovereignty, promises, and trustworthiness of God provide a foundation for life and action without equivalent in any other area of education. "The fear of the Lord is the beginning of wisdom: and the knowledge of the Holy One is understanding." (Proverbs 9:10) Because of its importance, SAU emphasizes and reinforces the application of theological and spiritual disciplines, both in academics and in cocurricular offerings.

The general education curriculum also includes requirements that represent the liberal arts: a broad cross section of how the world is known. In each discipline, four key elements are explored: the scope of the discipline, the terms of discourse in that discipline, the means of analysis in the discipline, and the significance of the discipline. Through these four elements, undergirded with Christ as the perspective for learning, students learn how the discipline contributes to human flourishing and how it displays God's attributes, activity, and glory.

The broad liberal arts approach builds students' confidence in their ability to engage with a variety of academic topics and disciplines and see similarities and interconnectedness throughout the scope of God's creation. Skills and foundational knowledge gained through liberal arts courses prepare students for more in-depth and applied study, and give them the ability to see beyond the topics and skills discussed in their major curriculum to deeper knowledge and broader perspective.

In addition to developing valuable professional and interpersonal skills, students often during this process discover interests and passions that enrich their lives. The exploration of ideas from the perspective of Christ teaches students far more than how to engage with information. It deepens their faith, fosters the development of wisdom and integrity, and equips them to interact with God and others in a meaningful way. The breadth of preparation and engagement indicative of a liberal arts education provides a strong, rich core through which nutrients flow, providing support and structure to the branches and leaves of the major curriculum, then producing fruit of professional and personal excellence that allows students to be critical participants in the contemporary world.

The University has established student learning outcomes for the general education program that provide a common focus and mechanism to align the varied components of knowledge found within the variety of the liberal arts disciplines. The general education outcomes allow for ongoing assessment of the learning process to ensure effectiveness and impact. The outcomes below were developed by the faculty committee that focuses on general education (the CPLA committee: Christian Perspectives in the Liberal Arts) in the spring of 2023.

Student Learning Outcomes for General Education

1. Demonstrate mastery of the fundamental components required for a foundational knowledge of the central liberal arts disciplines.

2. Demonstrate understanding of the major ideas and practices of the Christian faith (as attested in Scripture) to engender personal spiritual growth and an awareness of how various disciplines connect to Christian theology.

3. Demonstrate knowledge, skills, and appreciation for the diversity of human experience and cultures.

4. Demonstrate the ability to think about a subject in logical and ethical ways through the practice of analytical skills, such as attentive reading and observation.

5. Demonstrate the ability to write and speak in a responsible and compelling manner, using credible evidence to support conclusions.

Spring Arbor's Lifelong Learners in the Liberal Arts

Singer, Songwriter, Dove Winner: Babbie Mason, Class of 1978

Babbie Mason showed early interest in music. She started playing piano in her Baptist minister father's church at the age of 9 and became choir director shortly thereafter.

She began her post-Spring Arbor career as a school music teacher, first in Michigan, then in Georgia. Mason began her musical career in 1984, and in 1985 received first-place honors in both songwriting and vocals at the Christian Artist Music Seminar in the Rockies. In 1988, she signed her first record deal with Word Records in Tennessee. She went on to pen chart-topping singles, took part in 26 recorded music projects, and received two Dove awards. She has also written nine books and is active in Christian women's conferences. At Spring Arbor, Mason sponsors an annual songwriting competition and spearheads a scholarship for music students.

Artist, Muralist: Rick Herter, Class of 1984

Rick Herter began his career as a billboard painter and commercial artist before making the leap to aviation illustration by winning a national competition. In 1987, he became a participating artist in the elite Air Force Art Program, which allowed him to fly across the world to research his projects. His work has hung in the Smithsonian Air and Space Museum, the Air Force Academy, and the Pentagon. His corporate clients include Boeing, Rolls Royce, and G. E. Aviation. Herter holds the Guinness Book of World Records for the world's largest indoor mural, located at the Air Zoo in Kalamazoo, Michigan. In 2015, Herter painted a mural of Spring Arbor's history at the north end of the student center.

Scientist, Entrepreneur: Robert Gould, Class of 1976

Robert J. Gould received a bachelor's from Spring Arbor University and a Ph.D. from the University of Iowa. He completed postdoctoral studies at Johns Hopkins University. Gould joined Fulcrum Therapeutics as president and CEO at the time of the company's launch in 2016, bringing more than 30 years of experience to the role. Prior to that, he served as president and CEO of Epizyme from 2010 to 2015. Prior to joining Epizyme, Gould served as director of novel therapeutics at Broad Institute of MIT and Harvard from 2006 to 2010. He spent 23 years at Merck, where he held a variety of leadership positions, culminating in the role of vice president, licensing, and external research. During his time at Merck, Gould was instrumental in advancing more than 20 compounds from discovery into clinical development in multiple therapeutic areas.

Traditional Student Educator: Garnet Hauger

Garnet Hauger, then Garnet Smith, completed her bachelor's and master's in mathematics at Illinois State University and came to Spring Arbor as a mathematics instructor in 1971. In 1973, she was promoted to Assistant Professor, and four years later became Chair of the Natural Science Division. Hauger expanded her teaching repertoire by earning a further master's in statistics and probability from Michigan State as well as a PhD in Education Psychology. In 1989, she was celebrated by the campus students for "Teaching Excellence" and soon became a full professor and Dean of the School of Arts and Sciences. She retired briefly in 2008, when she received the SAU "Keeper of the Concept" award. Shortly thereafter, she was induced to return as an adjunct professor until 2023, when she was selected as "Adjunct of the Year." She is a superb example of a lifelong learner and lifelong teacher.

Nontraditional Student Educator: Natalie Gianetti, Class of 1978

In 1974, Gianetti came to Spring Arbor College to complete a degree she had begun working on 10 years earlier. While a student at Spring Arbor, she worked in the physical plant department as a Maintenance Secretary and Transportation Scheduler. In 1979, Spring Arbor began to offer courses and degrees at the Southern Michigan Prison near Jackson. In 1980, Gianetti became North-South Complex Coordinator in the prison education program. Spring Arbor established its first off-campus degree completion program in 1982, and Gianetti immediately joined that effort in prior learning assessment. In 1991, Gianetti was named Dean of Spring Arbor's adult higher education programs. After several name and course changes, the adult studies programs extended to 18 sites in Michigan and Ohio. Gianetti continued as Dean of adult programs for 20 years, during which thousands of nontraditional students had been enabled to accomplish their academic ambitions in multiple disciplines.

Nontraditional Student: Sheila Brown-Burrell, Class of 1996

Sheila Brown-Burrell began her studies at Spring Arbor as a student in our prison education program, completing a BA in Social Sciences with a concentration in Psychology. She subsequently earned a Master in Pastoral Counseling from Ashland Theological Seminary and a Doctor of Ministry degree from United Theological Seminary. She is a credentialed minister with the Church of God as well as a certified Advanced Alcohol and Drug Counselor. For some years, she was Director of Women at Teen Challenge of Detroit and now serves as Director of Life Challenge Mental Health Services in Detroit.

Nontraditional Student: Sandra Stephenson, Class of 2014 and MSW of 2016

Stephenson served simultaneously in multiple agencies in Jackson County, Michigan as a school social worker and mental health therapist. Her clients included very young and elementary-aged children, adults with severe mental illness or cognitive impairments, families, people of low economic status, and the elderly. She assisted patients in addressing illness, adoption, divorce, and unemployment. She is now Assistant Professor of Social Work at Spring Arbor University and oversees our students' internships, an important part of their professional preparation for licensure.

INTERDISCIPLINARY PROGRAMS

MedSAU

MedSAU was a collaboration between Spring Arbor University and the Brachial Plexus Palsy Clinic of the University of Michigan's School of Medicine. Faculty and students collaborated with clinic members in projects engaging Nursing, Health and Exercise Science, Natural Sciences, Education, Psychology, Social Work, and Business. The collaboration resulted in several internationally peer reviewed publications and presentations, including by Spring Arbor undergraduates.

CASE: Center for Autism Spectrum Enrichment

Founded by Psychology professor Terri Pardee, Class of 1986, CASE offers weekly social, emotional, and educational enrichment to as many as 40 K-8 students on the spectrum. Their families are also assisted. These services have been provided annually by up to 60 Spring Arbor students from majors including social work, psychology, youth ministry, drama, art, education, special education, and pre-physical therapy.

TOTAL COMMITMENT TO JESUS CHRIST AS THE PERSPECTIVE FOR LEARNING

To set forth more specifically the implications of total commitment to Jesus Christ as the perspective for learning,

Spring Arbor faculty and administrators produced a series of books on The Concept (see References), setting forth both the principles behind The Concept and in-depth essays on Christ as the perspective for learning the various disciplines taught by Spring Arbor University. This series is commended to all.

Educational applications of our total commitment to Jesus Christ are set forth immediately above, but our total commitment extends to our entire community. Spring Arbor's spiritual life is everyone's responsibility, but organizationally it falls within the Spiritual Life Programs, which is designed to encourage everyone to shine in the light of Christ. Everything we do is rooted in faith. Together, we worship in Chapel, both physically united or streamed to our remote members, study Scripture in small groups and engage our local community and the world through outreach ministries. Our journeys are unique, but our faith is shared.

Twice-weekly Chapel services bring our community together for an hour of worship music, prayer, and hearing the Word. Though Chapel is required for students living on campus, most students say attending Chapel is one of their favorite parts of life at SAU. Our Chapel Band is student led, and we also offer a Gospel Choir that performs in multiple venues. Our speakers are pastors, entrepreneurs, professors, and missionaries who are handpicked by our Chaplain to bring their message to our community. Previous and live Chapel services are available at <u>youtube.com/springarboru</u>.

Supplementing the weekday worship services is a once-weekly "chapel after dark" called DEEPER, during which a student brings the message and students worship and pray together. Student spiritual advisors are available in each of our campus housing units to support informal spiritual-growth opportunities. There is also a yearly weekend-long, off-campus spiritual retreat open to all students as well as a western ranch-based leadership retreat for athletes.

Spring Arbor seeks to strengthen our faith by living in our community. An outpouring of our faith is meeting the needs of our neighbors. We want to share the light of Christ by meeting those needs locally and globally. Among our service activities are:

Action Jackson: A mentoring program that connects two college students with "at-risk" children from the Jackson area.

American Red Cross Club: This club will promote the SAU concept as the last part of our concept states that our community will provide "critical participation in the contemporary world." As Christians, we are called to serve, and that is the mission behind the Red Cross. From actual blood donors to the volunteers setting up and recruiting donors, the idea is to serve people in this world. The beauty of this type of servanthood is that participants are helping someone who they don't know and probably never will. It shows the good in people and provides hope to many families.

Interfaith Shelter: This ministry travels to the Jackson Interfaith Shelter twice a week. They meet on Tuesdays and Thursdays outside the President's office at 6:15 p.m. and arrive back on campus by 8:45 p.m. At the shelter you will meet a wide variety of residents.

Project L.O.T.: Project L.O.T. exists to help SAU students to serve the Least of These (LOT) in Jackson, Michigan, through acts of service, discipleship, and organizing to meet physical needs. Project L.O.T. has a handful of standalone programs such as Under The Lights, where SAU students engage in street evangelism in downtown Jackson.

Relay for Life: After cancer hit home for SAU students when a beloved chaplain and an SAU student were diagnosed with the deadly disease, Spring Arbor students and staff banded together to organize a Relay for Life event on

Spring Arbor's athletic track. This event now takes place every spring.

Spring Break Mission Trips: For some students at Spring Arbor University, spring break is a lot more rewarding than relaxing. Each March, SAU sends 100 to 200 students all over the nation to serve on missions trips. In past years, students have traveled to Mexico, Atlanta, Puerto Rico, Texas, Kentucky, New York City, New Orleans, Las Vegas, Panama Beach, the Navajo Nation, and Hamtramck, Michigan.

Wellspring: Two groups that consist of singers and instrumental musicians travel to camps throughout the summer to lead worship. The group is selective. Auditions are required to be a part of Wellspring.

Spring Arbor University people's total commitment to Jesus Christ

Missionary to China: James Hudson Taylor III, Class of 1949

James Hudson Taylor III was the son of Free Methodist Missionaries who served in China. His family was interned by the Japanese in Weihsien, the same camp where Eric Liddell was held. After the family was released at the end of

World War II, Taylor returned to the United States and to Spring Arbor College, from which his father had graduated. After graduation, he pursued further education at Greenville College, Asbury Theological Seminary, and Yale University. In 1955, Taylor and his wife, Leone Tjepkema, a fellow Spring Arbor student, began their missionary service in Taiwan. Taylor became president of the newly founded China Evangelical Seminary in 1970, and from 1980 until 1991 was president of the Overseas Missionary Fellowship, originally founded by his great grandfather as the China Inland Mission. In 1993, he joined with others to form Medical Services International, which he led for 10 years. For this work and his longstanding concern for the people of China, Taylor received honorary citizenship from Sichuan province.

Missionaries to Burundi, Central Africa
Betty Ellen Cox, Class of 1936

Her life career was serving as a missionary in central Africa for 35 years, specifically Rwanda-Burundi. She participated in the finalization of the translation of the Old Testament into the Kirundi language and compiled the first Kirundi-English dictionary. Cox also founded and administered several mission schools. She was consulted by the government in developing a complete program of studies for all primary schools in the country and participated in approval of candidates for schools of higher learning. She also translated the Free Methodist Discipline as well as other books into Kirundi. Upon her return to the United States in the 1960s, she continued to serve her mission field by translating a year's supply of Sunday School lessons for Burundi primary schools.

Gerald Bates, Class of 1953

After Spring Arbor, Bishop Bates attended Asbury Theological Seminary and was appointed by the General Missionary Board of the Free Methodist Church to Central Africa in 1957. He distinguished himself as a missionary, evangelist, educator, and administrator, first in Burundi and then in war-torn Zaire. After being forced to leave a dangerous area, his family returned as soon as possible to resume their ministry. Bates supervised the translation of the Bible into the Ebenbe language and prepared Christian education material in Swahili. He also directed a Theological Education program by extension in Zaire. He served as area administrator for Central Africa from 1975 to 1985, when he was named a Bishop of the Free Methodist Church. He also served as the President of the Free Methodist World Fellowship from 1989 to 1995 and President of Spring Arbor University from 2007 to 2008.

Healthcare Entrepreneur: Jacob Atem, Class of 2008

Jacob Atem was one of 40,000 children orphaned by the Second Sudanese Civil War. He was one of Sudan's "lost boys." When he was 6 years old, his parents and several siblings were killed by northern Sudanese Arab militias. After walking more than 2,000 miles with other lost boys, he found refuge in Kenya before coming at age 15 to the United States and a foster family who encouraged him to complete high school and to attend Spring Arbor University.

According to CCCU President Shirley Hookstra in naming him the 2019 Council for Christian Colleges and Universities Young Alumni of the Year, it was at Spring Arbor that he experienced "the antithesis of his lost boy experience: a welcoming community of faith, full of mentors and friends ready to invest in his life." Jacob Atem continued his education and while still a student cofounded the Southern Sudan Healthcare Organization (SSHCO), of which he is now President and CEO. SSCHO's clinic in Jacob's hometown now sees more than 3,000 patients monthly at a cost of less than $5 a person. He graduated from SAU "prepared not only for graduate work, humanitarian work, and global advocacy, but ready to serve our world as an ambassador of Christ, as a minister of redemption and reconciliation, and as a critical participant in the contemporary world."

Critical Participants in the Contemporary World

Spring Arbor University seeks to prepare all members of our community to be critical – that is, important, influential, significant – participants in the contemporary world wherever they may find themselves. We do this in the first instance through our academic programs, the breadth of which is indicated by our eight schools:

Gainey School of Business
School of Communications, Media and Fine Arts
School of Education
School of Engineering
School of Humanities
School of Natural Sciences
School of Nursing and Health Sciences
School of Social Sciences

CROSS CULTURAL STUDIES

To ensure an awareness of other cultures, we provide a program of Cross Cultural Studies. A basis of intelligently participating in the affairs of the contemporary world is to realize that we are no longer an isolated people but part of a global community intimately linked to the rest of humanity and the world. This vague notion only becomes reality when there is actual interaction with those different than us.

A further impetus to Cross Cultural studies is that Christ's incarnation on earth was probably the greatest cross-cultural experience of all time, moving from the perfect presence of God to fellowship among Adam's fallen race. Christ was an "Asian-born baby ... who became an

African political refugee" before he was two years old. He moved freely among various ethnic and cultural groups (Jews, Gentiles, Samaritans) as well as different social classes. Christ Himself modeled numerous cross-cultural interactions throughout His ministry on earth. Besides Christ's example, the entire Bible gives accounts of God's people interacting cross-culturally throughout history.

Spring Arbor's cross-cultural studies include a semester on campus studying the culture or cultures to be visited in terms of five major social institutions – economics, education, family, government, and religion – and the cultural elements by which those institutions are articulated – architecture, fine arts, music, artifacts, language, crafts, leisure activities, and eco-diversity. This is then followed by a visit to the countries or distinctive communities studied led by experienced faculty members. International destinations for students in 2023-24 include Costa Rica, Guatemala, Morocco, Greece, England, Scotland, Bulgaria, Cambodia, Nepal, Czech Republic, and Israel. U.S. destinations include McAllen, Texas; Chicago; and southern Florida.

We also encourage students to consider a semester abroad within their program. These options include Oxford, England; Tokyo, Japan; Strasbourg, France; Amman, Jordan; and Seville, Spain. There are scholarships available for several of these destinations.

BRIDGING THE GAP

Beyond cultural awareness, a key skill necessary to being a critical participant in the contemporary world is the ability to "bridge the gap" between differences in cultural, religious, political, and many other perspectives. The "Bridging the Gap" program initially ran in January 2020 and resulted in students from two institutions with significant ideological differences finding common ground with their peers. Students at Oberlin College – known as a bastion of liberal thinking – in Oberlin, Ohio, are sometimes labeled as elite, intolerant "snowflakes," while SAU students are sometimes labeled as conservative, intolerant "evangelicals." Each is supposed to view the other as the irreconcilable opposition. The goal of the "Bridging the Gap" program was to challenge that notion by facilitating conversation between students from the schools.

"Bridging the Gap" was introduced to SAU through Simon Greer, a nationally recognized entrepreneur and social change leader. The program began with simple yet profound guidelines for its participants: "The intention is to take seriously the things that others hold dear. If it matters to them, then it will matter to us; we will not try to convince anyone that they are wrong or change them; and rather than thinking we are diminished by listening carefully to ideas we might disagree with, we will trust that we are enhanced by it."

Students learned and practiced skills such as listening, providing feedback, and telling their stories. They explored each other's values, worldviews, political ideas, faith traditions, and much more. Students were encouraged to hold to their convictions and not to blur differences or seek watered-down compromises. Elizabeth Stewart, a senior communication studies major from SAU, said, "We knew the course was a safe space to learn and a safe place to disagree. Greer designed it around hearing others' perspectives and made sure we were set up to be curious, listen, agree, disagree, and focus on intellectual humility." Recently the Nantucket Project released a film highlighting the program's success, which can be found on YouTube. Nineteen campuses now participate in Bridging the Gap.

SAU Chief Diversity Officer Kevin Brown spoke in front of the White House at the United We Stand Summit to discuss the importance of the Bridging the Gap program at SAU. The Summit was hosted by President Joe Biden to "bring together Uniters from across America who are leading work in their communities to build bridges and address hate and division." Greer and "Bridging the Gap" have secured funding to continue SAU's partnership with Oberlin College and expand the program thanks to the Arthur Vining Davis Foundation and Templeton Religious Trust.

"I believe that we have to be committed to breaking down barriers and eliminating harmful bias, discrimination, and racism so that we can create a campus community that truly reflects the depth and breadth of God's kingdom," Brown said. "By participating in 'Bridging the Gap,' we were able to offer students the opportunity to learn from others and practicing active listening — two invaluable steps on the road to developing authentic relationships that will lead to trust, honesty and respect.

SPRING ARBOR UNIVERSITY CRITICAL PARTICIPANTS

A few examples among many

Education: Recently recognized Spring Arbor graduates in education:

- Jonelle Hasselback
  - Special Education teacher for the Cognitively Impaired at Jackson High School
  - Special Education Adjunct at Spring Arbor University
  - Jackson Magazine's Top 5 Educators for 2023
- Jeremy Patterson
  - Assistant Superintendent for Secondary Curriculum at Jackson Public Schools
  - President, Michigan Elementary and Middle School Principals Association
- Sarah Anderson
  - Second-grade teacher at Warner Elementary
  - Spring Arbor University

- o Teacher of Year (Jackson Magazine) in 2022
- John Williams IV
  - o Currently SAU Assistant Professor and Women's Basketball Coach
  - o Formerly Principal for Addison Elementary
  - o Former Teacher at Jackson Public Schools
  - o Nominated for Regis and Kelly Teacher of the Year
  - o Named Michigan Hero in Education while at Addison
- Tracey Lowder
  - o Superintendent at Vandercook Lake Schools
- Tiffany Adema
  - o English Teacher at Northwest High School
  - o Jackson Magazine's Top 5 Educators in 2022
- Shannon Tinkle
  - o Northwest Elementary
  - o Jackson Magazine's Top 5 Educators in 2022

Educational Counseling: Terri Tchorzynski, Masters in School Counseling, 2010

Terri Tchorzynski is a Professional School Counselor at the Calhoun Area Career Center (CACC) of Battle Creek, Michigan. She was honored as the 2017 National School Counselor of the Year by the American School Counselor Association (ASCA). Under Tchorzynski's leadership, CACC received national recognition as an ASCA model program (RAMP). In Michigan, Tchorzynski was named the 2016 Michigan School Counselor of the Year. She was a top presenter at Michigan Department of Education's Career and Technical Education Conference, and an Honorary Counselor of the Michigan School Counselor Association.

Lawyer, Educator: Glen Winters, High School Class of 1925

Glen Winters graduated from Spring Arbor Seminary when he was 15 years old, but finances prevented him from pursuing his further education immediately. He did manage to attend the University of Michigan for law and was admitted to the bar in 1937. In 1956, he was appointed as Executive Director of the American Judicature Society and served in that position for many years. The Society is an independent, nonpartisan membership organization working nationally to protect the integrity of the American justice system. Winters was also one of the organizers of the Christian Legal Society in Michigan. An observer at the time remarked on how he exemplified The Concept at the highest level of his profession, and another commented that he was devoted to the Lord Jesus Christ and a steadfast Christian. In 1975, the Society published Glen Winters' *Handbook for Judges*.

Law: Dale Stephenson, Class of 1979

After graduating from Spring Arbor, Dale Stephenson went to the University of Michigan Law School and became a distinguished environmental attorney and international legal consultant. For most of his career, Stephenson served as a general partner with the global law firm Squire Sanders (now Squire Patton Boggs), where he focused on the Middle East region, environmental law issues, and complex dispute resolution for more than 30 years. Dale recently completed six years as Chairman of the Board of Trustees of Spring Arbor University

Politics: Mary Taylor Previte, Spring Arbor Junior College AA, Class of 1951

Mary Previte, daughter of missionary James Hudson Taylor II, came to Spring Arbor, which her father had attended, after liberation from a Japanese concentration camp during World War II. At 14, she lost her left hand in a revolving saw accident but continued her studies, which included a BA from Greenville College and a MA from Rowan University in New Jersey. She was the Administrator of the Camden County Youth Center for more than 20 years and was elected in 1997 as the first female president of the New Jersey Juvenile Detention Association. In 1998, she was elected to the New Jersey General Assembly and served there until 2006, when she chose not to seek reelection.

Politics: Renell Weathers, SAU site-based Bachelor in Business, Class of 2009

Weathers was a Community Liaison for Lily Missions Center prior to becoming a casework manager for Michigan State Senator Mark Schauer. In 2009, she became Schauer's

Senior District Representative during his tenure in the United States House of Representatives, and in 2011 became Community Engagement Consultant for the Michigan League for Public Policy, which she still serves.

Business: Les Dietzman, Class of 1962

Les Dietzman began as a teacher but eventually steered toward the retail industry. His intention was to do the will of God and always to conduct business using Christian principles. After beginning with the J.L. Hudson Company in Detroit, Dietzman worked for Dayton-Hudson for 20 years before moving to Ames department stores, where he was Executive Vice President of Sales. In 1990, he moved to Walmart Inc. Shortly thereafter, he was persuaded to lead Family Christian Stores and did so for 10 years. He also served as Spring Arbor University's Chairman of the Board from 2003 to 2010.

Business: Don Walker, Class of 1978

After graduating from Spring Arbor, Walker joined Rockwell Automotive in finance. His interests shifted toward logistics, and after a very brief association with Ryder Integrated Logistics, he began a 15-year association with Coopers and Lybrand as a supply chain consultant. One project was assisting Eli Lilly in launching a new Alzheimer's diagnostic, which was of interest to Walker because his mother had passed away from the disease. This project then led to a long-term career with Eli Lilly. In addition to Walker serving as a Spring Arbor trustee, his family has been a generous donor to Spring Arbor's housing and athletic facilities.

Healthcare: Chad Noble, site-based Spring Arbor business degrees, 1999 and 2005

After his first graduation from SAU, Noble went to work for Allegiance Health – now Henry Ford Allegiance Health – in Jackson, Michigan, and served there for more than 21 years. In 1998, he became a member of the leadership team as Director of Governmental and Corporate Affairs. He was also President of the Allegiance Health Foundation from 2012 until his recent retirement. He continues to consult on health care management issues.

Nonprofit Management: Gregory Bontrager, Class of 1983

After his Spring Arbor major in psychology and minor in business, Gregory Bontrager pursued his Master of Administration from Western Michigan University in 1986. Bontrager served as the President and Chief Operations Officer of the American Cancer Society, Inc., Worldwide, one of the world's the largest nonprofit organizations. He was one of the senior executives who led the organization through what was arguably the most significant transformation of a nonprofit in U.S. history. Bontrager was a Trustee of Spring Arbor University from 1995 to 2007 and again from 2017 to the present. He is the current Chair of the Board of Trustees.

THE CASE FOR THE
CHRISTIAN COLLEGE

Dr. David L. McKenna, President of
Spring Arbor College, 1961-1968

A COMMUNITY OF LEARNERS

Spring Arbor University is 150 years old. Its longevity is matched only by its faithfulness to the mission for which it was founded. Today, that historic mission is defined by the Spring Arbor Concept. Even though The Concept was written 60 years ago, its theological, academic, and societal roots go deeply into the soil of the institution's founding in 1873. Contrary to the popular notion that all meaningful history can be collapsed into the "Radical Now," the Spring Arbor Concept celebrates the past, energizes the present, and gives hope for the future.

Imagine then, this Introduction as a panoramic screen on which we see the past 150 years as perspective for the current and future case for the Christian college as written by the Spring Arbor University of today. The thought of a sesquicentennial history has its own intrigue, but when the story is framed by our Christian faith and our Wesleyan distinctive, our anticipation reaches new heights. Add then, the fact that Christian higher education is going through a time of testing for its integrity, its relevance, and its influence in a secularized culture and skeptical academy. With its calling sure and its Concept clear, Spring Arbor University does not flinch at the test. The confidence is not arrogance. Too many worthy institutions of Christian higher education have succumbed to the subtle or obvious onslaughts from academic, governmental, economic, and cultural opposition. In fearless response, Spring Arbor University attests its case with the humility of dependence upon the will of God for its continuity and its effectiveness.

I come to the 150th anniversary of Spring Arbor University from a personalized perspective. When I calculate the number of years in which I have been a part of the Spring Arbor experience, I surprise myself. At the beginning of the sesquicentennial year of 2023, I celebrated 75 years, half the Spring Arbor history, as a person intimately related to the school in a variety of contexts. After beginning in 1947 as a student, I advanced to alumnus, professor, dean, vice president, president, trustee, and chair of the board. Today, I carry the honored titles of President Emeritus and Chair Emeritus. During these 75 years, I have also had the privilege of being part of a forward movement from a high school and junior college to a four-year college and now a university.

Readers will have to forgive me if this Introduction sounds like a love letter. I owe so much to Spring Arbor over the years that I cannot help but let my gratitude show through in everything I write. At the same time, if longevity counts, I should have a perspective of our institution's history that spans the years, reinforces the roots, examines the present and energizes the future. Along the way, permit me the favor of an elder citizen who flavors his writing with personal anecdotes that serve as both mirrors for the past and windows for the future.

My love for the Spring Arbor Concept knows no bounds. Written while riding backwards in a college station wagon at high speed on I-94, I have been ready to live and die for it, not just because it qualifies as the mission statement that defines the very existence of the University, but because it has proven its value for strategic planning and tactical operation in both curricular and cocurricular spheres. Moreover, it fulfills the prophetic promise of bringing together the vision for a culture of being, believing, and doing in a single statement. Now, I want to recognize the instrument through which The Concept becomes reality. It is found in the concise statement that identifies Spring Arbor as a "community of learners."

Community is defined by our relationships with God, self, and others through Jesus Christ that create a sense of belonging, a spirit of wholeness, and a surety of hope.

Given this definition, the meaning of community at Spring Arbor University stands apart as an inspired instrument through which grace flows, transformation continues, and The Concept comes to life again and again.

Since the time that The Concept was written, the importance of "community" in the academic setting has risen to a level of urgency, if not crisis. The culprit is a culture that exalts "The Radical Self" at the expense of the spiritual and social relationships so essential to community. Robert Bellah has defined The Radical Self as "each of us doing our own thing for our own good." Disaster is the outcome. Under the hubris of The Radical Self, the scene in the Garden of Eden is being rerun. Once again, in their contemporary image, Adam and Eve are becoming God and reworking the decisions of authority, identity, and belonging. Consequently, our relationships, whether with God, self, or other humans, are collapsed into The Radical Self with crushing consequences. Spurred on by the viral pandemic, we are rapidly becoming a lonely people, lacking meaning and losing hope. Standing firm against this tide, the "community of learners" at Spring Arbor University is the antidote for the ills of playing God and belonging only to Self. Centered in Jesus Christ as the perspective for learning, we dare to claim a community of belonging, reconciliation, wholeness, and hope for the learners at Spring Arbor University.

A COMMUNITY OF BELONGING

As a freshman at Spring Arbor Junior College in 1947, I knew nothing about the history of the school or its sponsoring denomination, The Free Methodist Church. More than that, I did not know a single soul on the campus. Our freshman orientation began with a story told by Charles Kingsley, Director of Field Services, who, each weekend, blanketed the Free Methodist churches across Michigan and Ohio with student musical and preaching teams. Charles began his welcoming speech with his oft-told story.

In 1873, the Reverend E.P. Hart, later a bishop of the Free Methodist Church, and his wife, Martha, were forging their way west on a missionary journey that included a stop at Spring Arbor, Michigan. They were greeted by the sight of a defunct college campus. Earlier missionaries had ventured from Otterbein College in Ohio to found a new institution at the small and safe village of Spring Arbor. In hopes to expand in larger village with more citizens to contribute to the school's endowment, the college was restarted in Hillsdale, Michigan. Episcopal Methodists came next, also failed, and moved their institution to Albion, Michigan.

Hillsdale College and Albion College thrived in their new settings with Spring Arbor bearing the stigma as a graveyard for the Christian college.

Perhaps with this memory in mind, Reverend and Mrs. Hart stepped off the train in a nearby village. Except for the tracks, the train depot, and a nearby farm, the area was almost devoid of buildings and homes.

Still, when Mrs. Hart viewed the scene, her eyes reflected the vision of the Spirit of God and her own steely grit as she vowed,

> "While there's a track, I'll never look back, but
> go on at the risk of my all."

The Reverend's wife foresaw a line of history that has now extended for 150 years. Yet, her words are as fresh and true today as they were when she spoke them. The pioneering and missionary vision has never been lost. Consequently, when we look back on the story of Spring Arbor University, we do not just see a series of historical events merely as sequences in time. We see a "movement" that flows forward through the years as an unbroken line energized by the leadership of His Holy Spirit. A movement is a phenomenon all its own. Yes, it has moments marked by significant events, but in every highlighted happening we can feel the forward thrust perceived and predicted by Mrs. Hart. So, as God called the Children of Israel to "remember" the bondage of Egypt and the freedom of Sinai, He also calls Spring Arbor to be a "community of belonging" with lament for our shortcomings and doxology for our successes. Our lament is as essential as our doxology to our life story. In both deeply felt expressions, we are being guided by the Spirit of God toward the maturity of mission and the fulfillment of His purpose. The movement, in each case, is always forward.

Our lament begins with the story of early Free Methodists as dauntless pioneers forging their way westward across the unsettled American continent. At strategic points on their journey, the Spirit called them to stop, build their homes, establish their church, and found their college. It is the integral "community of belonging" among these three institutions that gives Free Methodism its distinction. The sense of "*our* homes, *our* church, and *our* college" is a divinely given relationship for which there is no substitute. At the same time, Free Methodist pioneers never nursed the fear of loss to outsiders. Evangelism along with a love for the common good prompted our forefathers to invite all those who might benefit from our sense of belonging, especially those in poverty or under oppression, into the company of our homes, churches, and schools. For good reason, then, the march of ministry forward across the nation shows us founding more colleges – Roberts, Greenville, Spring Arbor, Wessington Springs, Central, Seattle Pacific, and Los Angeles Pacific – than a small denomination can logically sustain. Logic may fail, but no one can criticize the motive or the level of academic standing that the colleges have achieved over the past 150 years.

Our lament is found in the fact that we now tend to think of our homes, churches, and schools as self-sustaining and separate institutions. Is this another intrusion by a secular and self-belonging culture that drives us apart? One indicator may be the declining numbers of Free Methodist students in our educational institutions. Another indicator may be the stagnant numbers of church membership in North America over the past 50 or more years. Still, another indicator may be the lack of an identifier that binds us together with our homes, churches, and schools. If ever we needed connectors among home, church, and school in a community of belonging it is now. Radical self-interest is taking its toll of our connections in community and wreaking havoc with our sense of belonging. Add the dehumanizing impact of advancing technology along with the isolation of a pandemic. Out of our desperation, we join social tribes and political factions that only increase the divisions between us and leave us lonelier than ever. Existential loneliness now plagues us as much or more than the viral pandemic. Our lament comes as an impassioned appeal for a Free Methodist Church initiative that foresees our homes, churches, and schools, not as separate institutions but as a divinely inspired and holistic system of belonging in Jesus Christ on which we will pledge our future.

"Praise God from Whom All Blessings Flow" is the doxology that more than matches our lament. From every human predictor, the educational institutions of the Free Methodist Church should have died or become stagnant long ago. Instead, the relational line of genius in the leadership of trustees, administration, faculty, staff, and alumni has kept them alive, well, and growing as genuinely Christian institutions. Furthermore, they have continued to move forward with the same steely vision of Mrs. Hart. Spring Arbor University is certainly one of the leaders in the advancement of our educational mission in which every student is welcomed to our "community of learners" – and more.

I am witness to this truth. As noted earlier, when I arrived on the Spring Arbor campus in 1947 as a college freshman, I did not know the name of any other student. My two roommates were World War II veterans with an outlook far different than an 18-year-old kid. To top off my lonely start at the college, I had no knowledge whatsoever of the Free Methodist Church. In fact, I had been cautioned against its alleged liberalism, not just in matters of dress and demeanor but in the loss of high-spirit revivalism and the doctrine of Holiness. So, after freshman orientation, I walked alone to the Ormston Hall dining commons for my first meal. Tables for eight were set for family-style dining with either a faculty or staff member serving as our host or hostess. As we ate, my loneliness increased as I listened to the chatter of other students about their exploits at youth camp that summer. After the meal, however, devotions began with a spontaneous chorus. When the familiar strains of "Jesus Is the Sweetest Name I Know" echoed through the dining hall, the spirit of family took over, and, for the first time, I felt at home. My faith in Christ and the sense of belonging to the Spring Arbor family became one in a relationship that continues until this day.

Not long ago, I received a letter from a Spring Arbor alumnus who had just retired from his career as a military chaplain. He wrote to say thank you for his learning experience at Spring Arbor. As a freshman from Jackson, Michigan, he said that he was one of two Roman Catholic students on campus. Without understanding or experiencing the religious claims of the campus, he said that he felt like an outsider – until he went to Sunday dinner in Ormston dining hall. Each Sunday he noted that the President and his wife and children joined with the students in family-style dining that included a prayer and song. For the first time, he too said that he felt as if he belonged to the family. Out of that connection, he was transformed. He gave his life to Christ and followed the call to ministry as a military chaplain. In his letter, he just wanted to say thank you for the connection that gave him a sense of belonging and changed his life. His testimony verifies the fact that the sense of belonging at Spring Arbor, anchored in our relationship with Jesus Christ, is transformative. It is also the keen edge of differentiation that sets Spring Arbor apart in the company of higher education.

Our mission is no longer limited to the compact college on a single campus with its family feeling. Virtual learning, distance learning, extension centers, and graduate studies are all challenges to the transformative sense of belonging for the Christian university. Do we really believe that a "community of learners" is essential to the mission of Christian higher education? Dare we claim that the transformative community is the keen edge of differentiation among institutions of higher education? If so, how do we create that sense of community in a high-tech world that tends toward separation more than belonging, individualism more than community, and efficiency more than transformation? In this question we have come upon the crux for the significance as well as the survival of the Christian college for the future. Without the evidence of a community where belonging brings transformation, the value of Christian higher education is short-changed. To create and nourish the personal touch and sense of belonging in the community of learners is as vital to the future of the Christian university as our mission statements and our strategic plans.

When the final history of American higher education is written, it must include the story of Free Methodist schools that not only survived the tidal of wave of public higher education and the tsunami of secularism but stood out above the flood with integrity as witness for their claims. The "community of learners" at Spring Arbor University is the fertile soil in which The Concept takes root and grows. With a sense of transformative belonging being nurtured in every participant and through every learning experience, on or off campus, one can hear a chorus singing the doxology, "Praise God from Whom All Blessings Flow."

A COMMUNITY OF WHOLENESS

Two life-changing moments highlight my learning experience at Spring Arbor Junior College. One came through the chapel address of Bishop Leslie Marston, an accomplished scholar as well an outstanding preacher and leader. As the text for his address, the Bishop chose Paul's appeal to his colleague, Timothy, whom he had left to minister at Ephesus while the Apostle moved on to Thessalonica. In a personalized appeal, Paul closes his letter by asking Timothy to *"Bring the books, and especially those made out of parchments." (II Timothy 4:13).* Bishop Marston went on to make the case for Christian higher education. He refuted skeptics who charged Christians with anti-intellectualism and reiterated the commitment of Free Methodists to academic excellence within the context of a Christian liberal arts college. Having come to college from a religious climate that aligned intellect with skepticism, I felt all the thrills of a great awakening and pledged from that moment on to give myself to the pursuit of learning in Christian higher education.

My other life-changing moment came in the course Introduction to Theology taught by Dr. James F. Gregory, President of Spring Arbor Junior College. After leading our way through the fundamentals of orthodox Christianity, Dr. Gregory introduced us to the distinctives of Wesleyan theology. He began by talking about the doctrine of Entire Sanctification, also identified as Holiness or a Second Work of Grace. To illustrate our lesson, he reached to the shoulder of his blue serge suit, found a tiny extruding thread, pulled it out and stretched it between his fingers.

> "Do you see this thread? Even though it is small, examination will show that it has the texture and tone of the whole cloth. In the same sense, when we are sanctified every fiber of our being will have the tone and texture of the whole will of God."

Coming from a church where holiness was an emotional event marked by the dread of piecemeal standards, I sensed an overwhelming thirst for the experience Dr. Gregory described. Even more, for the first time I glimpsed the beauty of holiness expressed in the wholeness of Christian higher education, not just in our individual lives but in every facet of the climate, curriculum, and culture. In a very real sense, this is where the Spring Arbor Concept was born.

As we have already noted, Spring Arbor Seminary came into existence at a watershed moment in American education. From 1716, when Harvard College was founded, until 1860, American higher education was dominated by colonial colleges offering a classical curriculum in the liberal arts and serving primarily the professions of clergy, law, and medicine. In 1862, however, Congress passed the Land Grant bill that established state universities focused upon technical fields of "agriculture and mechanical arts." The bill was consistent, not just with societal changes toward secularism, urbanism, and industrialization but also with the loss of dominance by the colonial college, the classical curriculum and select professions. In the academy, as well, the perspective of Enlightenment thinking came into vogue. Reason took over for revelation as the source of authority; technical studies pressed for priority over the liberal arts as the core of the curriculum, and career outweighed character as the outcome for learning. Even more decisively, teaching and learning in the public college and university moved rapidly toward a smorgasbord of curricular and cocurricular experiences. Now, 150 years later, the movement toward technical studies has been sealed with Jacques Ellul's diagnosis of "efficiency" rather than "meaning" as the expected outcome for American higher education. If so, the revolution is almost complete. Competence replaces character and productivity triumphs over personhood. "Wholeness," with its meaning for learning and living, is lost in the shuffle. Sad to say, many Christian colleges have defected from the faith and become lost in the backwater of the changing tide. Others have kept the claim but lost the spirit. Almost all of those who kept the faith have survived to live another day.

Spring Arbor University is our case in point. Based on the Spring Arbor Concept, there is no doubt about the underlying commitments of the University. All scholars and learners are expected to be engaged in the outworking of personal faith in Jesus Christ as <u>the</u> perspective for learning, serious study of the Christian liberal arts and professional studies, and critical participation in the contemporary world. Even today, I count the time working together with the Spring Arbor faculty to develop The Christian Perspective in the Liberal Arts curriculum in the early 1960s as the most meaningful of learning experiences. Every facet of the curricular and cocurricular climate felt the effect of integrative courses in the liberal arts and professional studies. Modules of the Sophomore Exploratory Experience, Cross Cultural Studies, and the Senior Seminar served as complements to make the curriculum truly whole. Highest credit goes to our current administrators, faculty, and staff for continuing to infuse the University with the lifeblood of The Concept. Word is that a recent accrediting team included in their final report the commendation for a campus on which every student they met could cite and explain the Spring Arbor Concept to the visitors.

With equal vigor and understanding, we need to communicate the theological position on which The Concept and its "community of learners" is based. As we have already noted, Spring Arbor is thoroughly Wesleyan in doctrine and practice. Central to that theological position is the doctrine of Holiness or Entire Sanctification as a means of grace. Our contention is that the outworking of Holiness is wholeness, not just in our personal lives, but in our primary institutions as well. Consistent with Dr. Gregory's illustration of the blue serge thread, we must assure that every aspect of our believing, being and doing is consistent with the will of God, the mind of Christ, and power of the Holy Spirit. Wholeness is not Holiness, but if we are holy, we will be whole. Most important of all, if Spring Arbor University qualifies as a community of learners seeking the truth, it will be the wholeness of truth guiding our search and confirming our discoveries. A triad of truth leads the way for us.

As Christian scholars, teachers and students, we begin with the conviction that all knowledge is in the Father. From the first word of Genesis to the final word of Revelation, God the Father is attested as *"one God and Father of all, Who is over all and through all and in all."* (Eph. 4:6). Whether in the physical, human, technical, metaphysical, or spiritual universe, He is Creator of all, and all belongs to Him. Consequently, as the universe of knowledge expands into new and exotic dimensions, nothing is outside the realm of

His creation, His ownership, and His care. He is sovereign in Person, and His Word is Truth.

Next, as Christian scholars, teachers, and students, we give ourselves to the discipline that <u>all knowledge is One in the Son.</u> Colossians 1:17 is the text that specifies this all-encompassing truth: *"He is before all things, and in Him all things hold together."* To be whole, all truth of the Father must be centered in the oneness of the Son.

When the Christian Perspective in the Liberal Arts (CPLA) curriculum was being developed by the faculty, a question was raised about the wording in The Concept regarding the role of Jesus Christ in the learning process. Would we say that Jesus Christ was "a" perspective or "the" perspective for our learning. The answer makes a world of difference. If He is only "a" perspective, our Christian faith is only one of many centers. But, if He is "the" perspective for learning, He is also the center that holds all things together with meaning and wholeness.

Finally, as Christian scholars and teachers we see that <u>all knowledge is Whole in the Spirit.</u> As Jesus drew near to the end of his earthly ministry, He gave His frightened disciples the assurance, *"When He, the Holy Spirit, has come, He will lead you into all truth."* (John 16:13). In the beauty of this promise, we see the vision of the Holy Spirit as our teacher, leading us step by step toward the wholeness of truth in every sphere of life and love. The Holy Spirit never works alone but always in relationship to other persons of the Trinity, especially Christ, the Son. He also works in relationship with persons and processes. When He indwells our personhood, we become holy; when He infuses our processes, they become whole. In essence, this is what is meant by the integration of faith and learning in the Christian college and the primary reason for its existence. With All truth that is in the Father as His text, and with the Oneness of truth that is in the Son as His lesson plan, the Holy Spirit is the teacher of wholeness, the giver of holiness, and the maker of meaning. Whitman's "noiseless, patient" spider comes to mind. Like the spider weaving its web in perfect symmetry, the Holy Spirit noisily and patiently spins the filaments in every sphere of our lives into the perfection of the holy and the whole.

Let the carillon tower on the Spring Arbor University campus be our case in point for wholeness in the academic process. In the four pillars that form the base for the carillon, we can see a curriculum of wholeness dedicated to serious study of the Christian liberal arts and professional studies. Revelation, reason, tradition, and experience are the names on the four pillars. They represent the Wesleyan Quadrilateral or the four ways for knowing truth. When it comes to the search and discovery of truth in the academic setting, each of the pillars serves a vital function. But there is always the incumbent danger of revelation, reason, tradition, or experience becoming an exclusive force that overwhelms or eliminates all of the others. This is where the Holy Spirit becomes our guardian and our guide. It takes the synthesizing Holy Spirit centered in Jesus Christ to assure the integrity or wholeness of the Quadrilateral. By determining how the pillars interact in the search for truth and bringing them into critical balance, the Holy Spirit functions as mentor, monitor, and moderator for our intellectual task. Because revelation in the Word of God is ultimate truth, it can deny or confirm reason, tradition, or experience, but it does not stand alone. When the synthesizing Spirit is at work, all sources of knowledge come into concert with the whole will of God. Without apology, we Wesleyans speak about Spirit-filled scholars and teachers whose primary task is the integration of faith and learning in their competence as well as their character.

Then, let a recent experience confirm the work of the Holy Spirit bringing wholeness to us as persons. I was in the doctor's office for a physical exam. Prior to the doctor's entrance a nurse came in to review my medical history. When she sat down at the computer, I checked her identification badge to learn her name. The sight cannot be forgotten. She was wearing a gold badge on which I saw the words, "Spring Arbor University." How could a nurse wearing a Spring Arbor University name plate be in a Seattle, Washington, hospital serving a former President of the school?

An unforgettable story unfolded in that doctor's office. The young woman was a graduate nurse completing her degree as a Nurse Practitioner at Spring Arbor University.

Of course, my first, egotistical question was to ask her if she remembered the McKenna Carillon on campus? "No," she answered, "I have never been on campus!" Graduate study for the advanced degree in the cooperative program between Spring Arbor University and the University of Michigan was a natural fit for a person of her Christian faith and undergraduate degree in nursing. So, when she and her husband moved to the State of Washington to follow his career, she chose Kaiser Pemanente to complete her internship and earn her degree. The sight of the gold badge bearing the name "Spring Arbor University" is a doxology in itself. She and I joined together talking about "our" University as if we were lifelong friends. In her personal character, professional competence, and Christian faith I saw the Holy Spirit at work in making all things whole.

In sum, wherever and whenever we touch down with the Spring Arbor Concept in the "serious study of the Christian liberal arts and professional studies," we are called to find our role under the tutelage of the Spirit of God. A small thread from a blue serge suit then reminds us that with the command, *"Be holy as I am Holy,"* (Leviticus 11:44) comes the promise of holiness and wholeness.

A COMMUNITY OF HOPE

Every generation of Christians needs to stop and ask the question, *"If the Christian college did not exist, would it have to be invented?"* As harsh as it seems, this is the salient question facing Christians in America today. One hundred fifty years ago, the Christian college was counting on the "Passive Hegemony" of a quasi-Christian culture that still favored the dominance of the colonial college and its classical curriculum. By the mid-1950s and the post WWII period, however, the shift to public higher education was almost complete.

My doctoral advisor at the University of Michigan, Dr. Algo Henderson, chaired the Truman Commission of 1950 that produced the volume <u>Democracy in Action</u> with its plan for the future of higher education. Public universities were expected to dominate the academic landscape, and community colleges were to be free to every student. Only a handful of elite private colleges were expected to survive. In the 1970s, however, the surprise of the "Born Again" movement escalated Evangelicals into a "Popular Plurality" with powerful influence in conservative politics. Coming into that era, three-quarters of Christian colleges were predicted to die before the end of the decade. Instead, a resurgence of Christian higher education was evident in the cooperative ventures of the Christian College Consortium and the Council of Christian Colleges and Universities with 140 or more members.

Fifty years later, all has changed. How well I remember sitting on the platform at the 1982 National Evangelical Association when President Ronald Reagan gave his best-known speech condemning the Soviet Union as the "Evil Empire." A rousing, standing ovation sealed the status of Evangelicals in Republican politics, perhaps at the price of its future.

Somewhere, after Reagan's speech, Evangelicals began a rapid slide in public opinion toward a hard-nosed, right-wing position, allegedly aligned with white supremacy and political backlash on such critical issues as right to life, racial diversity, sexual identity, global immigration, and environmental protection. With the coming of the pandemic in 2020 and its ensuing symptoms of psychological alienation and social despair, Evangelical Christianity has lost more ground. Fewer persons are identified with the movement, churches are losing members, and most poignantly, more young people of college age are designating themselves as "Nones" when asked about their religious beliefs. Christianity itself is being pushed to the sidelines of popularity and power. Add the fact that the prevailing mode in the general public is a loss of hope. For the first time, the next generation does not feel as if its future will be better than the present. If these trends continue, the primary movement that the Christian college serves will be categorized at best as a "Prophetic Minority." Not unlike Israel in exile, Christians and Evangelicals will have to become adjusted to a minority voice sounding a prophetic note. Opposition, if not persecution, may well accompany the change. Rather than counting on a plurality position to assure enrollments, accredited status, academic freedom, endowment dollars, and government support, the Christian college will have to find its prophetic voice from a minority position.

Is the Spring Arbor Concept still valid as the guide for the Christian college serving a prophetic minority? We must turn to the Biblical model of exile for the answer. To be a prophetic voice from a minority position, the Christian college will have to speak the truth, take a risk, and sound a note of hope. Most delicate among these tasks will be to speak the truth to power, both inside and outside the church. As we have already contended, Allness of truth in the Father, Oneness of truth in the Son, and Wholeness of truth in the Spirit anchor The Concept to a biblical base that cannot be compromised. In fact, in the time of a prophetic minority, these truths must be sharpened for application to prevailing conditions. Biblical scholars in the Christian college will be expected to take the lead in drawing the focus for these truths, especially in the Oneness of truth in the Son, from whom "the" perspective for learning flows. Add then the outcomes after these truths are applied. Perhaps as never before, a sense of belonging leading to faith, a spirit of wholeness connected with meaning, and a surety of hope lifted by transcendence will be the expectations for the faith and learning experience. These outcomes will apply not just to the Christian college as an institution but also to the system of Christian higher education in whatever form it might take, whether virtual learning, satellite centers, weekend seminars, or other educational units yet to be created and employed.

"Critical participation in the contemporary world" will be at a crux point in the time ahead. First, our identity as Christians will stand out when we are no longer the majority or the plurality but the minority. Nominal Christians will fall away under the same test that hones the identity as those who are "in Christ." Second, Jesus Christ as the cornerstone of our faith will have to be tenaciously held against deviations of belief that still claim to be Christian, whether from the right or the left. Third, our witness from the minority position will be a risk that includes the cost of self-sacrifice. Spring Arbor University has excelled with its graduates responding to critical areas of human need, such fields as teaching, ministry, and other forms of social service. Their Christian faith expressed in a servant spirit is most compatible with these fields and the social setting of schools, churches, hospitals, and human-service agencies. In more recent times, the fields of business, health care, and high-tech industries have been added to choices of Spring Arbor graduates. While these careers involve a different kind of test for character and competence, Spring Arbor graduates are still recruited because of the qualities they bring to these positions.

The climate is about to change. Christian witness in a hostile society entails a risk that we have seldom known.

Graduates in the field of education may confront unseen prejudice because of their opposition to such teaching as critical race theory. Graduates in the field of nursing and health care may confront similar bias if they are called to participate in abortion or euthanasia. Stretch these thoughts out to the rapidly advancing field of artificial intelligence. Graduates may have to walk a fine line between freedom and control of the human will. To say the least, "critical participation in the contemporary world" will no longer be protected by the leftovers of a "Passive Plurality." Servanthood will still lead the way, but sacrifice and even suffering may be honors bestowed on us in the name and for the sake of Jesus Christ. Graduates of the Christian college who apply the Spring Arbor Concept in their careers as well as in their personal lives will quickly learn what it means to be in the "Prophetic Minority."

How then do we continue our witness in the name and for the sake of Jesus Christ? First-century Christians in Rome give us an answer. When a plague swept through the city and killed thousands of Romans, the blame was placed on the small sect of Christians. Instead of fleeing the city to escape death, Christ followers did what Romans themselves refused to do: They risked their own lives to go into the condemned areas and minister to those who had persecuted them. Without doubt, the spirit of self-sacrifice played a major role in winning Rome for Christ. Our answer for tomorrow is the same. As the prophetic minority, we must be ready to take a redemptive risk at personal sacrifice to sound a note of reconciliation in a broken world. Spring Arbor University has precedent in its history.

In 1967, the inner city of Detroit, Michigan, went up in flames. Race riots fueled the flames, and white citizens fled to the suburbs. At Spring Arbor College, the President's Cabinet sat down to ask, *"Our campus is known as 'The Quiet Cove of the Spirit.' What is our responsibility to our neighbors in the ashes of Detroit?"* Out of that session came a risky venture known as Riot Scholars. An Admissions and Student Development team went into the heart of the city to see if they could find 10 young black men whose chances for college had been lost in the flames of their city. Seven students were found who qualified for riot scholarships on our passive and peaceful campus where only two students of color were enrolled.

A humorous anecdote highlights the story of the Riot Scholars on campus. When I left the President's Office one day and started down the walk to Ormston Hall, I met one of the scholars named Roy Lee Manning. I greeted him, "Hello, Roy," as if we were lifelong friends. He responded with a scowl and said, "My friends call me 'Roy Lee.' All others call me Mr. Manning." Talk about a classical putdown for a presidential ego. There and then I learned how wide the gap that we had to bridge to achieve goal of a Spring Arbor education for Riot Scholars.

Added to that encounter with Roy Lee was the risk of reaction from the quiet, safe, and conservative community of Spring Arbor. Shortly after the arrival of Riot Scholars on campus, the village was shell-shocked by the murder of one of our residents, a female owner and proprietor of the local gas station. While searching for the murderer, the police found muddy footprints tracking through the ground floor of Ormston Hall. Once the news spread, the rumor quickly surfaced that the footprints belonged to one of the Riot Scholars who was the murderer. The story was completely false, but it revealed the risk of the program and the fears of the community.

Two of the Riot Scholars graduated from Spring Arbor College, three transferred to other institutions, and two dropped out. Was the risk worth it? The answer is in the ripples of redemptive risk that are still moving outward through to the present time.

After the program was initiated, the Michigan Legislature picked up the spirit and passed legislation for the Independent Colleges Opportunity Program to provide scholarships for needy students from depressed areas like the inner city of Detroit. Years later, Shirley Ort, a student leader at Spring Arbor during the Riot Scholar days, put that same spirit to work in her role as Assistant Provost for Scholarships and Financial Aid at the University of North Carolina. Shirley authored "The Carolina Covenant" as a breakthrough program in financial aid so that the neediest youth in North Carolina could attend the prestigious university and graduate without debt. Through The Covenant, Shirley administered more than $40 million annually in scholarship aid.

When Shirley retired, Governor Pat McCrory conferred on her The Order of the Long Leaf Pine, North Carolina's highest honor that was usually reserved for its citizens who were born and raised in the state. With the award, Shirley joined the distinguished company of Maya Angelou, Billy Graham, and Michael Jordan. In addition, university trustees had the American flag flown at the U.S. Capitol in recognition of her work. Today, The Carolina Covenant is the model for universities across the nation, addressing the financial needs of the most underprivileged students. All from a risky start with a redemptive outcome.

When Spring Arbor University takes a risk on the front edge of our Christian witness, we are right in step with our Wesleyan heritage. Who can ever forget John Wesley leaving the high pulpit of the established Anglican Church to preach to miners and millers in the open fields of the English countryside? Or who can ever deny our legacy of Francis Asbury traveling 260,000 miles on horseback to preach the Gospel on the Western frontier of Kentucky? In that same spirit, we inherit the inspiration of Mrs. Hart getting off the train near Spring Arbor, facing forward, and announcing, "While there's a track, I'll never look back, but go on at the risk of my all."

In each of these risky ventures, there is the resounding note of transcendent hope. When the Spirit of God shows us things to come, He affirms the "Not Yet" of His Father's redemptive promise. Do we fully grasp this promise? God entrusts the Christian college with the greatest resource in all creation – the bodies, minds, and souls of the future generation. The responsibility is awesome, but by grace, the hope is boundless.

Even now, I reaffirm my commitment to Spring Arbor whenever I think of a student named Paul Lynch. Paul was a young African American man from a Free Methodist mission in the impoverished ghetto of Shreveport, Louisiana. As the only black man on the campus at the time, Paul was quickly renamed "Jet" by his teammates on the track team, because he ran the dash with blinding speed. I knew Paul as his Dean of Men, English teacher, and debate coach. As his Dean of Men, I had to help him fend off co-eds who were attracted to his smiling eyes and handsome face. As his English teacher, I had to tutor him in grammar because of deficiencies in his Louisiana schooling. Taking a dare, I invited him to join the debate team. Paul accepted and became a member of the varsity. But I also remember the debate he lost for us when he prepared his case for only the affirmative side. When we cast lots and drew the negative side, Paul was speechless.

Tragedy almost ended Paul's education at Spring Arbor. One night Paul's dorm partners engaged him in a college prank that ended with serious injury to one of the students. Paul and his buddies came close to expulsion, but after appeal, President James Gregory allowed them to continue their education under strictest probation. As his Dean of Men, Paul had to report periodically to me.

Paul Lynch graduated from Spring Arbor Junior College and Roberts Wesleyan College, returned home to Louisiana, completed his bachelor's degree, and excelled *magna cum laude* in law school. His outstanding character and credentials soon earned him a fast track upward in the U.S. Attorney's jurisdiction until he was elected as Federal Circuit Judge in the Cado Parish of the State of Louisiana. In his mid-40s, Paul's reputation brought him speaking engagements at national law conferences. At one of those conferences, he was to be the featured speaker, but after a daily jog he returned to his hotel room and unexpectantly died of a heart attack. At his memorial service, the federal law community from both Louisiana and the nation gathered to honor a great man with a radiant Christian witness. The Honorable Donald Walker, Chair of the Shreveport Bar Association, summed up the eulogies given that day with the words, *"The hand of God didn't shake when He made Paul Lynch."* Let the story of Paul Lynch be told again and again because he represents the heritage of redemptive risk and transcendent hope that distinctly belongs to Spring Arbor University today and tomorrow.

****

I have made my case for the Christian college out of the 150-year history of Spring Arbor University and my 75 years as a recipient of its blessings. For the future, I see beyond survival to significance when I envision the Spring Arbor Concept activated in its "community of learners" who share a sense of belonging, a spirit of wholeness and the surety of redemptive hope. Admittedly, these impulses belong exclusively to the heartbeat of a primary institution that represents the Body of Christ in an academic setting. No other Christian ministry carries this distinction or this responsibility. With good reason, we can refer to the Christian college as a "vine of God's own planting." Therefore, to lose or weaken the ministry of Christian higher education is to cripple the cause of Christ. The answer is not outside the Body of Christ itself. To depend upon the fragile factors of enrollment growth, financial aid, academic status, legal protection, and endowment gains is not sufficient. We need to go back to our primary question: *"If the Christian college did not exist, would it have to be invented?"*

I have answered "yes" by contending that the Spring Arbor Concept is confirmed by the Spirit-given virtues of belonging, wholeness, and hope infused in a community of learners as a ministry that cannot exist without the presence of the Christian college. My contention is backed up by my personal experience at Spring Arbor University. It is the Christian college to which I belong, through which I sought to be whole, and in which I hold my hope. On that premise, Spring Arbor and I join an ancient hero who dared to claim, "Here I stand, so help me God."

21ˢᵀ CENTURY CHALLENGES
AND COMMITMENTS

O ver the past several years, three areas of challenge for Christian colleges have arisen. The first is shared with all of higher education: growing skepticism as to the cost and net value of the traditional college experience. Parents and prospective students increasingly evaluate post-secondary education in terms of its employment outcomes, and these concerns have heightened due to the national concern with student loan debt.

Beyond the financial pressures and need for careful stewardship arising from questions of the value of higher education, the second challenge is specific to higher education institutions predicated on the truth of the Christian faith and the authority of Scripture. Past decades have seen increasing legislative and judicial activism in furthering LGBTQ/SOGI challenges to traditional Christian credenda. These may lead to governmental pressure with respect to hiring, behavioral standards, operations, and control of facilities in accordance with religious convictions.

The third challenge is societal and generational. Surveys increasingly indicate that many young people no longer have so much as an unconscious reliance on the Christian cultural heritage of the past. Nor can it be assumed that even those students matriculating in Christian colleges have a firm grasp of the basics of the faith. Further, modern philosophy has attacked the notion of objective truth, leading to both relativism in thought and behavior and cultural and personal anxiety arising from having no firm place to stand. The following commitments are both a response to current challenges and a guide to faithful fulfillment of Spring Arbor University's Why and Concept.

CHALLENGE 1: EDUCATIONAL

HIGHER EDUCATION VALUE QUESTIONS

A growing skepticism to the cost and net value of the traditional undergraduate, residential "college experience" has become increasingly common in recent years. This skepticism has been increased due to the national conversation about student loan debt (and the potential for forgiveness of some federal loans). Further, the pandemic caused many to reexamine the personal value of their career and life choices, leading to the "Great Resignation." In 2021-22, more than

25 percent of high school seniors nationwide appear to have decided at a minimum to delay college.

Both parents and prospective students are increasingly evaluating post-secondary education in terms of its employment outcomes. Spring Arbor University's recent graduates report 98 percent satisfaction with their outcomes, but this is not the universal experience. One result of skepticism of traditional higher education has been increasing interest and enrollment in trades training rather than traditional liberal arts education. However, despite the interest in training in trades, even community colleges are facing significant enrollment shortfalls.

Just as online courses and Zoom modalities represented significant changes in how education is delivered, ubiquitous internet information and artificial intelligence, most immediately represented by ChatGPT and GPT-4, create questions as to the role and value of traditional instruction.

Finally, whether because of the Covid pandemic, or simply as revealed by the Covid pandemic, freshmen entering higher education are generally observed to be less prepared for serious academic work than were prior generations. The extent to which this is due to political influences within K-12 education, perhaps displacing traditional instruction, is a matter for debate. The lack of preparedness of our incoming students is not.

Competitive Pressures

Particularly in the Midwest, demographic trends are not advantageous for higher education. The projected "demographic cliff" of a possible 15 percent reduction in the actual number of high school graduates beginning in 2025 is in addition to significant reductions in the last few classes. This alone would create significant competitive pressures for schools such as Spring Arbor University that have traditionally enrolled most of their students from Michigan and to some extent the broader Midwest.

One new competitive challenge introduced by the pandemic is the great demand for labor, which has caused employers to make increasingly attractive offers to potential employees. Students may well see immediate opportunities to earn what they regard as significant money as more attractive than going to school. This is particularly the case as employers offer tuition assistance among employee benefits. Relatively few employees to date have taken advantage of these offers, and completion is delayed by the part-time nature of the efforts of those who do accept tuition assistance. So, employer assistance is not an automatic advantage to colleges unless there is a tight relationship between the employer and the school, and the employer encourages such studies, particularly for employees hired without degrees.

Some of the national education conversation has focused on the alternative of quick, targeted credentials versus traditional degrees. Employers have become increasingly open to evaluating job candidates by skills rather than degrees and in offering their own training options as well as funding more traditional programs as employee benefits. The result of the latter has increased attention to the specific expectations of employers for what their employees should learn.

The apparent willingness, most recently of large employers such as IBM, to give what seems to be preference for skills and targeted credentials over degrees changes the competitive landscape. Higher education now needs to defend or expand the category of its offerings to include such credentials or explicit skills demonstration.

The adoption during the pandemic by many colleges of distant, Zoom, online instructional modalities has encouraged greater competition in each of those modalities through which Spring Arbor serves many of its learners. This further exacerbates the issue of the "demographic cliff," because students who traditionally chose residential campus, face-to-face programs close to home now have the option of pursuing degrees and other credentials entirely online from remote institutions.

Meanwhile, nearly half of states now offer some form of "free college" despite the slowing of support on the federal level. Local "promise" programs also reduce the cost of initial college years, albeit sometimes tied to specific institutions. These trends represent three distinct challenges/

opportunities to four-year colleges: first, direct competition for early college years; second, competition for transfer students; and third, transmitting institutional values as they are important (as for a Christian school) to those transfer students.

COMMITMENT 1: EDUCATIONAL

Spring Arbor University is committed to providing to our students excellent instruction that meets our learners where they are when they come to us in disciplines of professional and personal interest to those students supplemented by traditional liberal arts leading to skills of critical thinking, communication, and collaboration most likely to adduce to career and personal success. Spring Arbor is also committed to offering cocurricular opportunities that provide guided experiences by which students may learn to apply their disciplines and skills to real-world situations. And we are committed to providing that education from a comprehensive, intentional, unequivocal, and unapologetic Christian perspective. As the Chairman of the Board of Gordon-Conwell Theological Seminary recently remarked when it moved from a suburban campus to downtown Boston: "Our mission is permanent. Our modality can and should change."

CHALLENGE 2: INSTITUTIONAL

FINANCIAL

The mirror image of the national conversation on the cost of college to students is the cost of instruction for higher-education institutions. Higher-education costs are subject to escalation by inflation as are those of other participants in the economy. For small, private universities with relatively small endowments, enrollment competition places significant pressure on net tuition revenue relied upon to fund operations.

POLITICAL

In the past 50 years or so, groups within American society have sought to reshape popular values in such areas as sexuality, including abortion, same-sex marriage, and transsexuality. In some ways, these efforts have followed some of Alinsky's "Rules of Radicals," in particular the rule to "go outside the experience of the enemy." Even though recent Barna and Pew surveys report that American view "evangelical" as a political description rather than a religious position, evangelicals have to a great extent actually failed to present the Christian alternative to the secular perspectives on life, marriage, family, and the right to freely exercise religious conscience.

Although recently Christians have increasingly sought to engage winsomely in the political sphere to oppose these trends, the past decades have seen increasing activism in the legislature and judiciary furthering the LGBTQ/SOGI political agenda (e.g., support for the Federal Equality Act; and expansion of Michigan's Elliott-Larsen civil rights to matters of sexual orientation). These efforts may well put increased governmental pressure on Christian institutions. These pressures might range over hiring, behavioral standards, operations, and control of facilities.

Also, increased litigation in these areas, as well as increased public sentiment on behalf of nontraditional positions concerning sexuality and related issues that might influence jury decisions, have caused insurers to reduce willingness to insure Christian institutions apart from any overt political action. Indeed, Spring Arbor University itself has had to change carriers after many decades with one provider who refused to continue to provide coverage for potential LGBT/SOGI lawsuits.

Further, recent years have seen efforts – although yet unsuccessful – at state and federal levels to disqualify Christian organizations from governmental policies and assistance available to their non-Christian peers. Although Christian institutions have sought only to be afforded the Constitutional and statutory right to have sincerely held religious conscience accommodated, failure to conform to bureaucratic requirements for social and behavioral requirements incompatible with Christian convictions has been challenged vigorously by opponents. Only strenuous efforts to preserve religious exemptions already existing in law based on the First Amendment of the Constitution have preserved such key circumstances as access to financial aid for our students. For smaller educational institutions reliant upon tuition revenues from students dependent upon governmental financial aid, this is potentially an existential challenge. One can envision circumstances of serious pressure upon Christian college to yield on convictions to survive as going concerns at the cost of relinquishing the mission and purpose for which they were founded.

COMMITMENT 2: INSTITUTIONAL

Spring Arbor University will manage its operations and finances in such a way to ensure, within the limits of financial and economic pressures, the long-term viability of our institution.

More importantly, in the face of political pressure to diminish our purpose to educate for Christ and His kingdom from the biblical perspective on learning, life, and society, we will continue to stand firm on our institutional purpose as consistently articulated and executed through our first 150 years. We make this commitment in dependence upon God and confident that He is able to uphold us in this effort. But should He choose for His own purpose and glory to allow external forces to make it impossible to continue as an intentional, unequivocal, and unapologetic Christian institution, we are prepared to cease operations.

CHALLENGE 3: SPIRITUAL

The fourth plank of The Concept states that Spring Arbor University itself seeks to be a critical participant in the contemporary world. As such, we recognize two broad areas of societal, spiritual challenge that need to be addressed by Christian higher education.

GENERATIONAL

It is a commonplace in sociological, political, and religious history to speak of a three-generational phenomenon. The first generation is those who have themselves investigated and as a matter of conviction adopted a particular moral, political, or religious stance on the basis of which they live. The second generation is comprised of those who have received their modes of thought and behavior from their parents but often without the same kind of personal experience and depth of commitment. The third generation then perceives the behaviors of the second generation to be without foundation and either attacks them as hypocritical or otherwise rejects their legacy, even though the third generation continues to be influenced, albeit unconsciously, by the assumptions and practices of the prior generations.

What appears to have happened in America today is that we now have encountered a fourth generation, one which is without even an unconscious reliance upon the Christian cultural heritage of the past. Surveys of young people find astonishing numbers of GenX-ers, for example, who not only have no clear impression of who Jesus is but in many cases are literally unfamiliar with His name. To say this is a challenge for Christian higher education is obvious, but more pernicious is the reality that this generation is now without any objective foundation on which to build their lives.

As a result, young people are vulnerable to great mental stress in the face of relatively minor disruptions that would easily have been absorbed by earlier generations with at least the vestiges of confidence in a benevolent university (if not a sovereign God). This is so pervasive than even young people raised in putatively Christian homes also find themselves bereft of comfort when normal challenges of life arise.

Philosophical:

Much of modern philosophy has attacked the notion of objective truth. Although relativism may begin with the comparatively benign assumption that what's true for me need not necessitate that it be true for you, relativism easily gives way to the assumption that "my truth" is a surrogate for truth itself. Since it is the fundamental human sin to exalt oneself and one's opinions and preferences above those objectively set forth by a creator, this drift not surprisingly holds sway in much of American society today. The difficulty is that human beings realize at a deep level that some facts of life, such as gravity, are objective. So, we seek to find an "objective" place to stand ... frequently choosing social consensus as that place. In fact, the lack of objective truth, standards, and guidelines make the appeal of "going along with the crowd" even stronger than the usual human affinity for social connection.

Some years ago, the American Society of Landscape Architects recognized with a "residential design award of honor" a student project that examined children's playground behavior in the presence of observable boundaries (aka "fences"). What the project found was that if there were clear boundaries, the children felt safe to explore further afield, albeit within the boundaries. When there were no boundaries, the children huddled around an authority figure (a teacher) or else sought to remain as close to each other as possible to feel secure. Is it too great a stretch to suggest that this is the behavior we observe today?

Ethical and societal decisions are increasingly made based on celebrities' opinions or of fashionable "in crowd" preference. Having rejected or forgotten about the genuine human identity of being made in the image of God, "identity politics" has become a powerful way of seeking security by allying oneself with a group, particularly one of seeming fixed boundaries such as race and so offering security. Social media "influencers" are more persuasive than genuinely knowledgeable persons. And, in any event, there appear to be fewer means to determine "genuinely knowledgeable" since that suggests an objectivity that current philosophy will not permit.

The reality of sin is no longer mentioned let alone contemplated. Individuals who now make their own truth, while comforted by socially acceptable virtue signaling, when encountering the evil that is part of the human experience conclude that it is brought about entirely by "oppressive" others, i.e., those who do not share one's identity or reference group. The result, as William Butler Yeats wrote a century ago:

> "Things fall apart; the center cannot hold; /
> Mere anarchy is loosed upon the world, / The
> blood-dimmed tide is loosed, and everywhere
> / The ceremony of innocence is drowned; /
> The best lack all conviction, while the worst
> / Are full of passionate intensity." (*The Second
> Coming.* 1920)

Commitment 3: Spiritual

In the Wesleyan tradition, the discipleship of young believers was viewed as the responsibility of three institutions: the family, the church, and the school. As the recipient of young people for whom catechism and serious instruction in the faith has not been part of their experience, Spring Arbor University views as an important function in its commitment to critical participation in the contemporary world the effort to ensure that doctrinal and faith deficiencies in our own learners may be addressed and remedied during their association with us.

More broadly, since it can easily be demonstrated that much of the philosophical underpinnings of society with which we now contend were either developed or popularized by secular institutions of higher education, Spring Arbor University commits (and urges others in Christian higher education) to seek means to speak the truth of the Christian faith and the Gospel of Jesus Christ into this increasingly pagan conversation. Left without effective intellectual opposition, the lack of family or philosophical foundations can only leave this generation vulnerable to active and passive rebellion against God and so to His just wrath against those who neglect the great salvation He has provided through His son Jesus Christ.

CONCLUSION

Gregory Bontrager, Chair of the Board of Trustees, Spring Arbor University

When the school that is now Spring Arbor University was established in 1873, its purpose was articulated by B.T. Roberts, the founder of the Free Methodist Church, as to "combine sound and thorough scholarship with careful religious training," specifically the Bible standard of Christianity, and to make that education available to all who desired it. As David Warner, the principal of Spring Arbor, stated in 1903, the school was to be a center of "holy influence and spiritual power ... [sending] forth men and women with trained minds, full of faith and of the Holy Ghost 'to contend earnestly for the faith once delivered to the saints.'"

For 150 years, as a purpose-driven and unapologetically Christian educational institution, Spring Arbor University has enjoyed God's favor. We take this seriously and are committed to obedience in our mission fidelity to seeking that continued favor.

We exist to educate for Christ and His Kingdom, to prepare our students to make a life as well as a living, and to produce Christ-centered, Kingdom-minded marketplace leaders for this and succeeding generations. We will win the next generations of Christ followers through the marketplace … that is, homes, businesses, schools, politics, and society. And that reality is what it means to be critical participants in the contemporary world, as our Concept envisions.

The Concept in its fullness, and particularly in its total commitment to Jesus Christ, is our mission. We guard it because it is precious and because it is at risk. It is at risk in a culture undergoing a near revolution in its philosophical and political underpinnings such that Christianity is no longer the default bedrock of our society.

Despite the old proverb that "methods are many, values are few; methods often change, values never do," we are living through a time of challenge and complexity, and without attention, methods can sometimes seem to trump values. That will not be so at Spring Arbor University.

To guard our precious purpose, we will use any ethical and legal means to continue to educate for Christ and His Kingdom. We are determined to preserve the past, to manage the present and to map the future. We will never forget our fundamental purpose, though we will respond to shifting and changing demands of our world. We are different today from the past because our world is different, but Spring Arbor's vision, idea, and purpose set forth in The Concept will not change, and what we have to offer has never been more important.

As we began and have been for 150 years, so Spring Arbor University shall continue to be, providing sound academic and Christian education, open and accessible to all who choose it, in service to God who has so wonderfully preserved us to this day.

References

Alinsky, Saul D. "Rules for Radicals". 1971.

American Society of Landscape Architects. ASLA 2006 Student Awards. https://www.asla.org/awards/2006/studentawards/282.html

Beebe, Gayle D., and Kulaga, Jon S, eds. "A Concept to Keep". 2003

Beebe, Gayle D., and Kulaga, Jon S., eds. "The Concept and the Sciences". 2007.

Beebe, Gayle D., Kulaga, Jon S., Overton-Adkins, Betty, eds. "Keeping the Concept". 2004

Ellis, Brent. "Grace and Truth". 2022.

Free Methodist Church Michigan Conference Minutes, 1871.

Kirk, Marshall and Madsen, Hunter. "After the Ball: How America will Conquer its Fear & Hatred of Gays in the 90's". 1989.

Roberts, B.T. "Christian Schools". Earnest Christian, 1884.

Snyder, Howard. "100 years at Spring Arbor". 1973.

Snyder, Howard. "B.T. Roberts and the Founding of Roberts Wesleyan College". 2022.

Snyder, Howard. "B.T. Roberts Up-to-Date Vision of Earnest Christianity". https://freemethodistconversations.com/bt-roberts-up-to-date-vision-of-earnest-christianity/

Snyder, Howard. "Concept and Commitment: A History of Spring Arbor University". Spring Arbor University Press, 2008.

Snyder, Howard. "Rooted in Mission: The Founding of Seattle Pacific University 1891-1916". Reedy Press, 2016.

Steenhuysen, Julie, *The Hugh White Story,* "Spring Arbor College is People: Annual Report 1982-83", pp 10-11.

Wesley, John. "Catholic Spirit" Sermon 39. http://wesley.nnu.edu/john-wesley/the-sermons-of-john-wesley-1872-edition/sermon-39-catholic-spirit

Wesley, John. "The Witness of our Own Spirit". Sermon 12. http://www.wordsofwesley.com/libtext.cfm?srm=12

Wesley, John. "The Works of John Wesley. Volume III". Zondervan Publishing House, Grand Rapids, MI.

Appendices

The Spring Arbor University Statement of Faith

We believe that human beings, men and women equally, are created in the image of God and are called to be his faithful stewards on earth. Although all people have become alienated from God and affected in every part because of sin, by God's grace all who truly repent of their sin and believe in the Lord Jesus Christ are justified by faith, and adopted into the church, the people of God.

We believe that repentance and belief in Christ are evidenced by commitment to a life of obedience to the authority and commandments of the Bible as interpreted through sound exegesis and a traditional biblical hermeneutic.

We believe that the value of human beings does not depend on their marital status, but that human families were established by God to perpetuate humankind and to provide a stable community for nurturing children in faith and righteous living. Marriage between one man and one woman is the instruction of the Bible for establishing families, and physical sexual expression is to be confined to that marriage relationship.

We believe that God not only counts believers as righteous, but that he makes them righteous; freeing them of sin's dominion at conversion, purifying their hearts by faith and perfecting them in love by his Spirit, and providing for their growth in grace through God's participation at every stage of their spiritual life, enabling them through the presence and power of the Holy Spirit to live a victorious life of righteousness, justice and practical usefulness.

We believe God's Kingdom promises to establish "a new heaven and a new earth, where righteousness dwells" (2 Pt.3:13 TNIV) and where resurrected believers will participate in God's everlasting Kingdom.

THE SPRING ARBOR UNIVERSITY COMMUNITY COVENANT

INTRODUCTION

As an academic community, Spring Arbor University is shaped by the Spring Arbor Concept and by the stated mission that grows from it. The University is a unique community because of these commitments and because it includes both campus students and many alternative education students through its various extension sites. As an educational institution, SAU seeks to be thoroughly Christian. This SAU Community Covenant affirms the University's Christian commitment and recognizes the diversity of its extended student body.

As part of its commitment to Christian integrity, the University affirms the same foundational standards for students, staff, faculty, and trustees. This Covenant, therefore, includes all these groups and serves as the basis for the more specific behavioral expectations required of campus students. Persons who become members of the SAU Community as trustees, faculty, staff, or students covenant to accept and model the Spring Arbor Concept as elaborated in this Community Covenant.

The Community Covenant includes biblical principles and Christian lifestyle affirmations which are central to our Christian identity and should be affirmed by all who affiliate with Spring Arbor University. It also includes specific community disciplines that help to create the kind of Christian learning environment desired by the University and envisioned by the Spring Arbor Concept.

BIBLICAL PRINCIPLES

The Bible provides basic principles for Christian character and behavior. These include the following:

1. Principle of LORDSHIP: Jesus Christ is Lord over all dimensions of life, thought, and culture. Jesus calls us to a life of faith and love including obedience to the moral teaching of the Bible and to responsible discipleship in all of life (Luke 9:23; Philippians 2:1-13; Colossians 1:10-23; Hebrews 12:1-3, 13:12-16; 1st Peter 1:13-16).

2. Principle of LOVE: Love for God and love for others are the primary motivations for Christian relationships and behavior. Scripture reminds us that "love is the fulfillment of the law" (Romans 13:10; Leviticus 19:18; Deuteronomy 6:4-6; Matthew 5:43-48; Luke 10:27; John 13:34-35, 14:15; Romans 13:9).

3. Principle of COMMUNITY: Community is central to the life of the University and its understanding of Christian education. Christian love includes mutual accountability and forgiveness within the community, as well as sensitivity toward others'

needs and weaknesses. It includes participation in the worship and activities of the church, which is a necessary context for Christian living (Matthew 18:20; Acts 2:42-47; Romans 12:9-21; Ephesians 4:25, 5:15-21; Colossians 3:12-17; Hebrews 10:24-25).

4. Principle of CHARACTER: God, through the Holy Spirit, places in every believer the inner resources to grow in Christian character and to minister to others through supportive relationships. The University community encourages an environment in which its members can grow in compassion, integrity, and the integration of faith and learning (Matthew 15:10-20; Romans 8:5-17, 12:1-2; Galatians 5:22-25; Ephesians 4:1-16; Philippians 4:4-9; 1st Peter 2:21).

5. Principle of RESPONSIBLE FREEDOM: God gives us the freedom to live responsibly within the framework of His Word. He calls us to pursue righteousness and practice justice and mercy toward everyone. Responsible freedom includes discipline stewardship in all areas of life and critical participation in the larger culture (Genesis 1:26-28, 2:15-17; Micah 6:8; John 8:31-36; Galatians 5:1 and 13-14; 1st Peter 2:16, 4:10-11).

CHRISTIAN LIFESTYLE

A lifestyle consistent with the above principles is expected of all members of the University community. Jesus calls and by grace assists us to practice Christian virtues and to avoid attitudes and actions that the Bible condemns as sinful. Members of the University community agree to exhibit such Christian virtues as humility, honesty, a forgiving spirit, self-discipline, faith, hope, and love. The University trustees, faculty, and staff seek to be role models to the students in the practice of these virtues.

Attitudes that the Bible condemns as morally wrong include greed, jealousy, pride, lust, bitterness, uncontrolled anger, and prejudice based on race or ethnicity, sex, or socioeconomic status. While these attitudes are not always obvious, they are as subject to God's judgment as are more visible sins. The Bible also condemns such behavior as drunkenness, stealing, profanity, unfair discrimination, dishonesty, occult practices, and extramarital sex.

Responsible freedom includes respect for the sanctity of human life and faithful stewardship of mind, body, time, gifts and abilities, finances, and the natural environment. It also requires thoughtful Christian discernment in matters of entertainment and associations.

COMMUNITY DISCIPLINES

In addition to the moral standards prescribed in the Bible, the University has adopted certain disciplines that are intended to foster a campus atmosphere consistent with the Spring Arbor Concept and with the University's Christian heritage. These disciplines embody such foundational Christian principles as self-control, avoidance of harmful practices, and sensitivity to the heritage and practices of other Christians and people of other belief systems. The University advocates abstinence from gambling, profanity, the illegal use of drugs, and the use of tobacco and alcoholic beverages. These community disciplines apply to trustees, faculty, staff, and all undergraduate campus students. They also apply to alternative education students, graduate students, and adjunct faculty whenever they are involved in University functions or using University facilities.

CONCLUSION

The University seeks through this covenant to cultivate an environment in which Christian character may flourish. The Covenant is intended to promote a lifestyle based on Christian principles and devotion to Christ. It affirms that living Christianly results from conscious choices rather than mere acceptance of prevailing practices. The University's larger hope is that the SAU community may in some measure model and point towards the kind of gracious, just, and peaceable society pictured in the biblical vision of the Kingdom of God.

Made in the USA
Columbia, SC
28 September 2023